Caesar's Census, God's Jubilee

Rethinking and Reimagining the story of Mary and Joseph's Journey to Bethlehem

By W. Scott McAndless

TABLE OF CONTENTS

Many of the ideas in this book have been with me for a very long time. They began to come together as I participated in and thought about the Jubilee 2000 campaign, an effort to raise awareness about the need to cancel the debilitating international debts of a number of developing countries. This noble campaign sought to take the debt cancellation, release and return policies of the Old Testament (particularly Leviticus 25) and apply them to the practical difficulties that were facing the poor and to the world's most highly indebted nations at the turn of the millennium.

But the campaign also did something else. It created a new awareness of the Biblical idea of jubilee in the churches that participated. And I remember being struck at the time by the idea that the celebration of jubilee could help to solve what I saw as some serious problems with Luke's account of the birth of Jesus. I even preached a sermon on that subject—linking Christmas to the idea of jubilee—on the Christmas Eve of 1999.

The idea gave me a new perspective on the familiar nativity story, but it was certainly not fully formed. Every year, as Christmas came around, I continued to think about it. When I saw pageants and other presentations of the Christmas story, and when I heard about the release of the film *The Nativity Story* in 2006, I was reminded of the inadequacies of the traditional interpretation of Luke's account and of the problems that are created by a careless blending of the stories as told in Matthew and Luke's gospels.

Then in the spring of 2008, while doing some reading on the uprising of Judas the Galilean, I discovered the final piece of information that seemed to make everything fall into place. I felt that I had to write down my thinking and spent the next few months—in whatever free moments I had—just typing my ideas into the computer. It was a process that I thoroughly enjoyed. Of course, as I wrote, I kept finding information that only seemed to confirm my approach.

Finally, I had my ideas all worked out. But there seemed to be something missing. I realized that I needed to do some dreaming and imagining. After all, for about two thousand years, Christians have been taking the basic nativity stories in Matthew and Luke's gospels and using their imaginations to add a myriad of details. They have brought all kinds of extra characters and situations to Luke's manger—things that had certainly never been imagined by Luke.

We have become familiar with stories that include an innkeeper at an important inn at Bethlehem, a donkey and an assortment of other animals gathered around the manger, a little drummer boy, camels, wise men and more.

In addition, the traditional interpretation of the story has been painted and drawn by some of the greatest artists who have ever lived, sung by some of the greatest singers and told by some of the greatest storytellers. A whole rich and well-populated world has grown up around the nativity story—a world so detailed that it seems very real even if much of it has little connection with the Biblical accounts. I realized that my theories weren't just an attempt to correct some misunderstandings about the Christmas story. My ideas would seem to attack that entire imaginative world that has grown up around the story over the centuries and would be resisted for that reason alone.

I realized, therefore, that it wasn't going to be enough to just put forward some new ideas; I needed to help people to imagine the story in very different terms. There is no way to compete with all of the great artists who have described the nativity, but I felt that I could at least point people's imaginations in some new directions. Therefore I began to use my own imagination. I wrote a series of little dramas (I call them interludes) to place between each chapter. These are not intended to be historical accounts of events that we know for sure took place around the birth of Jesus, but rather a kind of historical fiction inspired by Luke's account and informed by what I have discovered about that account while writing this book.

These interludes are not presented in chronological order. Instead they jump backwards and forwards in time. Usually they are imaginings that have been inspired by the ideas in the chapters immediately before or after them. I certainly don't mean to suggest that the only way to conceive of these events is as I have done it, but it is my hope that they help you to encounter Mary and Joseph in the historical setting that Luke describes to us. Perhaps it might even inspire some who are more talented than I to use their art to bring the story to life in new ways.

Many people have helped to inspire and improve this book. I am very thankful for the people of my congregation, Knox Presbyterian, Leamington and later at St. Andrew's Hespeler Presbyterian, who were happy to give a hearing to my strange ideas and who let me try out all kinds of different things. I particularly thank the Bible Study groups who worked through early drafts of this book with me chapter by chapter. Their wisdom and suggestions truly helped me to think through the implications of what I was writing.

Most of all I thank Dominique, Gabrielle and Zoé whose support in this project, as in all things, is invaluable.

Scott McAndless,
Cambridge, ON.
August, 2013

This map offers a possible route for the journey taken by Mary and Joseph described in Luke's Gospel. Bethlehem is about 70 miles (112 km) from Nazareth. Mary and Joseph's journey would have taken them a much greater distance as they went around geographical and political obstacles.

In the year 6 CE (when the census that Luke mentions was taken) Galilee and Perea were ruled by Herod Antipas, son of Herod the Great. Samaria and Judea were under direct Roman rule as part of the Province of Syria. The Decapolis was a semi-autonomous region dominated by ten Greek-style city states.

This map is licensed under the Creative Commons Attribution ShareAlike 2.5 http://creativecommons.org/licenses/by-sa/2.5

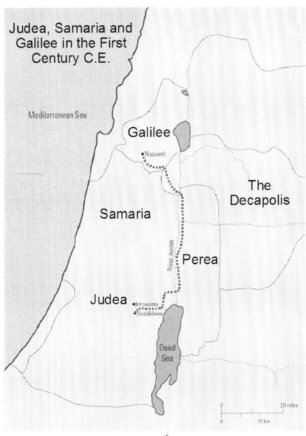

Two young people slowly make their way down the road. There is a man who is carrying a sturdy staff and he leads a donkey while a woman rides perched on top of the animal. The woman's belly is very round. She is obviously very pregnant and very near to her time to deliver. They have come a very long way and yet there is still a long and difficult road ahead of them. Though they are weary, they do not stop. They continue to trudge down that long and lonely road as evening falls.

Suddenly the woman places her hand on her belly and stifles a cry. She is struggling, coming to the end of her strength and she fears that she will not make it to their destination before the baby arrives.

Joseph looks back to see how his wife is doing—his face full of concern. She looks away, not wanting to let him see the tears that are beginning to form in her eyes.

"Mary," he says, "I know the way is hard, but we don't have any choice. We must make it to Bethlehem in time to register in the census there. It is the law. We may not like it but that is what the emperor has commanded and we must surely obey all earthly authorities. It is God's will that we do so."

"I know, husband," she replies haltingly—almost out of breath, "and I will find the strength I need to make it there."

"I know that you will. Let us continue on for a few more miles before we stop to rest."

The woman silently nods, biting her lip and they continue on their way. The night darkens and the stars begin to appear—one particularly bright and low on the horizon seems to lead them forward.

They move on into the gathering gloom.

1) The Journey from Nazareth to Bethlehem

The image of that traveling couple, Mary and Joseph, and their donkey is one of the most iconic in Christian tradition. It has appeared on more Christmas cards than anyone could ever count. It is a necessary scene in any Christmas pageant. What would Christmas be without it?

But what is the real meaning behind that journey from Nazareth to Bethlehem? The iconic image comes to us from a few verses in the second chapter of the Gospel of Luke:

> In those days a decree went out from Emperor
> Augustus that all the world should be
> registered. This was the first registration and was
> taken while Quirinius was governor of Syria. All
> went to their own towns to be registered. Joseph
> also went from the town of Nazareth in Galilee to
> Judea, to the city of David called Bethlehem,
> because he was descended from the house and
> family of David. He went to be registered with
> Mary, to whom he was engaged and who was
> expecting a child. While they were there, the time
> came for her to deliver her child. And she gave
> birth to her firstborn son and wrapped him in
> bands of cloth, and laid him in a manger, because
> there was no place for them in the inn.[1]

Of course, Luke doesn't actually describe much of the journey at all. He doesn't say what route they took, who they travelled with or what their mode of transportation was. He certainly doesn't mention a donkey! All of the details have all been left to the imagination. But none of that has stopped Christians down through the centuries from having a very clear idea of what that journey looked like.

But there is a much larger concern than just what that journey might have looked like. We need to understand what that journey

---

[1] Luke 2:1-7. Unless otherwise indicated, Biblical references are taken from the *New Revised Standard Version*, Division of Christian Education of the National Council of Churches of Christ in the United States of America, 1989.

meant to Luke, the evangelist who tells the story (for the Gospel of Matthew in its nativity story does not seem to be aware of any such journey). It obviously comes at a key moment in Luke's account. But is it, for him, just a convenient means of getting Mary and Joseph moved from Nazareth, where they live, to Bethlehem, where he knows that the baby must be born? Or is there deeper symbolic and theological meaning in the journey itself?

The traditional interpretation of this part of the story in the Gospel of Luke is that Mary and Joseph travel from Nazareth to Bethlehem simply because they have been ordered to do so. It has been commanded by the highest political authority in the world—by the Roman emperor himself—as a part of the census that he is conducting. The couple comply with the order even though it means travelling a great distance through dangerous territory and even though it must be particularly risky for Mary to travel so close to the time of the birth of her child.

Christians also see the hand of God working in this story—influencing events and even working through the emperor's decree in order to make sure that Jesus is born in the right place and at the right time so that the scriptures may be fulfilled. This is the position of faith and it is undoubtedly also part of Luke's understanding of the events. But such manipulation apparently only goes on behind the scenes. It does not even require anyone's cooperation. Open obedience in this story is given only to Caesar, not to God.

Mary and Joseph's compliance with the order to travel to Bethlehem seems to indicate a willingness to submit to the authority of the emperor. Even if they only make the journey grudgingly and out of fear of what the consequences of disobedience may be, they are acknowledging that Caesar has enormous power over their lives, their movements and their actions. Therefore the journey, traditionally understood, would seem to be a perfect illustration of the principle we find in the First Letter of Peter:

> For the Lord's sake accept the authority of every
> human institution, whether of the emperor as
> supreme, or of governors, as sent by him to punish
> those who do wrong and to praise those who do
> right.[2]

Is that really the only lesson that we should take from this story—that we must learn to obey all human authorities at all times? Is that really what Luke intended for us to understand? Or is it

---

[2] 1 Peter 2:13,14

possible that there is a different way to look at and understand this long trek from Nazareth to Bethlehem?

To answer that question, we need to look more closely at the historical situation behind this passage. Jesus must have been born sometime around the turn of the era—when the dating system that we use today crossed from BCE to CE (or, to use the older dating system, from BC to AD). Let us review some of the key events that we know took place in Judea and Galilee at that time.

The entire region was ruled, up until 4 BCE, by King Herod the Great. Herod was a Roman client king, which is to say that he ruled as a king, but only exercised power on behalf of Rome and depended on Roman troops and influence to maintain his position.

Rulers of Judea at the turn of the era

Herod the Great	Archelaus	Direct Roman Rule
4 BCE	6 CE	

Herod's reign ended with his death in 4 BCE, at which time the Romans broke up his kingdom. The territories of Judea and Samaria were given to his son Archelaus who did not, however, inherit the title of king but rather the lesser title of *ethnarch*.[3] The territories of Galilee and Perea were given to another son, Herod Antipas, along with an even lesser title of *tetrarch*.

Archelaus's rule over Judea and Samaria did not go well and eventually, in 6 CE, the Romans stripped him of his power and exiled him to Gaul far off in the western reaches of the empire. Rather than replace Archelaus with another client king or *ethnarch*, the emperor decided that it was time for Rome to take direct control over the administration of Judea and Samaria, and so the territories were incorporated into the Roman Province of Syria. Galilee and Perea, however, were still being adequately ruled by Herod Antipas, and they remained what the Romans called a *tetrarchy*—essentially a smaller client kingdom—under Antipas's control.[4]

---

[3] Matthew mentions this succession in 2:22

[4] See H. Jagersma, *A History of Israel from Alexander the Great to Bar Kochba*, Fortress Press, Philadelphia, 1985 p. 118.

In 6 CE Emperor Augustus also appointed a senator of consular status named Quirinius as governor of Syria. As a part of the integration of Judea and Samaria into Syria Province, Quirinius conducted a major census of the region and also imposed a new head tax (Latin: *tributum capitis*).[5]

All of these events are well attested in the historical records and are not disputed. When we try to fit Luke's story of the birth of Jesus into this history, certain problems arise with his account. Let's take a closer look at some of those problems.

WHO IS IN CHARGE OF JUDEA?

The date of the birth of Jesus is usually given somewhere between the years 8 and 4 BCE. This date is based primarily on the account of the birth of Jesus in Matthew's Gospel. That gospel makes it very clear that the birth took place during the reign of Herod the Great. Indeed, Herod is a key character in the story. This means that Matthew is saying that the latest possible date for the birth of Jesus is 4 BCE. There is also the suggestion in Matthew 2:16 that Jesus could have been up to two years old when Herod sent his soldiers to Bethlehem to kill him. In saying that Herod ordered his soldiers to kill every boy in Bethlehem under that age, Matthew suggests that Herod learned from the magi that the boy in the prophecy could have been that old. All this has led to the idea that Jesus must have been born sometime around 6 BCE.

It is hard to reconcile that dating to the account of the birth of Jesus in Luke's gospel. There is absolutely no indication of Herod having any sort of power or authority in Luke's account. There is a brief mention at the very beginning of the account of Zechariah, the father of John the Baptist, serving as a priest during the reign of King Herod,[6] but once we get into the account of Jesus's birth, we only hear about Roman authority. Of course, Herod the Great did rule Judea as a Roman client king. Any power he exercised was always considered to be in the service of Rome. But while he lived, he was the visible head of government and was a ruler of such power and ruthlessness that no one could ignore or forget him. It is odd, to say the least, that Matthew's gospel could see Herod as such an overwhelming presence on the political scene at the time of the

---

[5] Ibid. p. 119.
[6] Luke 1:5

birth of Jesus, but that Luke should mention almost nothing about him.

Luke's reference to a universal census creates a number of problems. If indeed Caesar Augustus did decree that all the world—which surely must mean all of those parts of the world that were under Roman jurisdiction—should be registered at once, there would be abundant records of such a decree and the resulting census. The Romans were very good at keeping such records and Augustus was never slow to trumpet his military and administrative accomplishments. In fact, there is absolutely no record of any such universal census.

The Romans were very keen on taking censuses. In the ancient Republic, the position of censor was highly esteemed. When Augustus became emperor, he assigned the power of censor to himself and so any census taken was necessarily taken under his authority. The census was essential to many aspects of Roman society, politics and military affairs. In Rome itself, it seems to have been primarily about sorting the people into their tribes and centuries for the purposes of voting, as well as establishing eligibility for various public offices. To be able to sit in the Senate, for example, you had to prove to the censors, not only that you had the right ancestors, but also that you owned sufficient amounts of property and wealth.

Outside of Italy, the census was primarily about what Rome could get out of the people of its provinces. It was about creating rolls for taxation and about identifying able-bodied men who could be recruited for service in the legions and the auxiliaries, although the latter did not apply to Jews who were exempt from military service.

The census was a vital administrative tool for the Romans. The rolls would have been renewed in the various provinces and regions on a fairly regular basis by key administrators moving from place to place. But it is unimaginable that the empire could have had the resources to undertake a census of its vast territories all at once!

Surely, Luke and his early readers would have understood this. They were far more familiar with matters of imperial administration that affected local populations than we are. Therefore it seems reasonable to assume that, when Luke writes, "In those days a decree went out from Emperor Augustus that all the world should be registered,"[7] he means something different than that Augustus decided to conduct one census of the entire empire all at once.

He might be referring to something that we know *did* happen. When, in the year 6 CE, Judea was incorporated into the Province of Syria it officially became part of the Roman world in a way it had never been before. It came under direct Roman rule and administration for the first time.

When Luke refers to a decree of Caesar Augustus that all the world should be registered, he could be referring, not to a particular decree given at one time that a universal census be taken, but to something more like a standing order—that all parts of the Roman world should have adequate census records. Since censuses were being taken in all parts of the Roman world under the authority of the emperor, there was doubtless some such standing order. Such a decree would apply to Judea, however, only when it officially became part of the Roman world in 6 CE. At this moment, therefore, the *first* census would be taken and that is exactly how Luke refers to it: "the first registration... taken while Quirinius was governor of Syria."[8]

Indeed, we do know that a major census of the area was undertaken at exactly that moment. It is described for us in *Antiquities of the Jews* by the first century Jewish historian, Flavius Josephus:

> Quirinius, a Roman senator who had ascended
> through the magistracies up to the consulship and
> also enjoyed high dignity in other ways, came to
> Syria at this time, with some others, sent by Caesar
> to judge that nation and assess their property. A
> man of equestrian rank, Coponius, was sent with
> him, to take full charge of the Jews, though
> Quirinius came into Judea too, which was now
> annexed to Syria, to assess their property and
> dispose of Archelaus's money.[9]

That certainly sounds a lot like the census that Luke is referring to in his gospel—right down to the important role played by Quirinius, the governor of Syria Province. In fact, once we

---

[7] Luke 2:1

[8] Luke 2:2

[9] Josephus, *Antiquities of the Jews*, 18:1-2. Emphasis added. (All passages from Josephus are taken from Patrick Roger's 2007 translation found at http://www.biblical.ie/josephus.)

understand what he is saying, we discover that Luke seems to have a very firm grasp of the political situation that prevailed in Judea in the year 6 CE and that he is saying that Jesus was born in the midst of it. This creates a large problem in that the census that Luke seems to be referring to occurred nine years after the death of King Herod and possibly eleven years later than the date of Jesus's birth as recounted in Matthew's Gospel.

QUIRINIUS

Luke also states that Jesus was born while Quirinius was governor of the province of Syria and this statement creates similar problems with his account. As we see in the passage from Josephus above, Quirinius was indeed the governor of Syria with jurisdiction over Judea as well. This clearly did not happen until 6 CE, almost a decade later than the death of King Herod and so creates a big conflict with Matthew's story.

This is a problem with Luke's account that has long been recognized. Down through the centuries there have been many attempts to resolve the issue of the governorship of Quirinius. Several have suggested that he may have served as governor twice and his first time in office corresponded with Herod's reign (though governors certainly did not normally serve two separate terms in the same province). There is also some evidence that Quirinius could have served in a different magistracy in Syria prior to being named governor in 6 CE and some have suggested that Luke may be referring to a role in governing rather than his actual position as governor when Jesus was born.[10]

So there have been a number of efforts to make Quirinius's governorship coincide with Herod the Great's reign so that Matthew and Luke might be in agreement about the date of the birth of Jesus. I will not attempt to engage in any of those arguments now. I will take the position that the most obvious reading of Luke's mention of this Roman governor, based on the known history of Syria Province, indicates that Luke is saying that Jesus could not have been born any earlier than 6 CE, which makes it rather difficult to harmonize Luke's and Matthew's nativity story.

---

[10] E.g. F. F. Bruce, *The New Testament Documents: Are They Reliable?*, Eerdmans, 1981 (1943), pp. 86-87.

A Roman provincial census was all about helping the empire to exploit the resources of its provinces, especially through taxation. The point of it was to create reasonably accurate rolls that indicated what people had and where they could be found in order for the Roman tax gatherers to do their work. Because of this, it only seems reasonable that any census should be taken in the town, city or administrative district where people actually lived. This is how censuses are taken to this very day—and the census takers are often very careful to make sure that responses are given only in a person's primary residence. This was also the common Roman practice.

The writer of the Gospel of Luke seems to indicate that the census he is speaking of was taken in a very different way. He suggests that everyone was registered, not in their place of residence, but in their ancestral home. This makes no administrative sense and there is no evidence that the Romans ever took a census in such a manner.[11] In fact, it would seem that a census taken under the circumstances that Luke describes (in the midst of a mass migration of people) would yield data that would be useless for the purposes of the Romans. This is another major problem with Luke's account.

Some Christian commentators have sought to respond to this problem by pointing out that there is some evidence of a Roman practice where individuals who owned property in another jurisdiction were required to return to that place in order to pay tax on their property there. I. Howard Marshall suggests, for example, that Joseph could have owned some property in Bethlehem and been required to go there when the census was called,[12] but there are two problems with that explanation.

First, it does not account for the kind of mass migration of people that Luke mentions. "All went to their own towns to be registered," seems to mean, in the context, that everyone went to their ancestral homes, but surely *all* the people did not own land in those places!

---

[11] Some have cited a decree of C. Vibious Maximus of 104 CE which required absentees to return to their home towns to be registered in Egypt. But the requirement in this case is to return to a primary place of residence, not an ancestral home. See Raymond Brown, *The Birth of the Messiah*, Doubleday, 1977. P. 396.

[12] I. Howard Marshall, *The Gospel of Luke*, William B. Eerdmans Publishing Co, 1978. p. 101.

Secondly, Luke does not offer any indication that Joseph owns any land in Bethlehem. Indeed, he indicates the contrary. When Mary and Joseph arrive in Bethlehem, there is no place for them to stay and Mary is forced to lay her newborn baby in a feeding trough. If Joseph were the absentee landholder returning to the place from a distant country and if he had a wife who was about to deliver, how could the couple not be given at least a room in which to stay?

If Bethlehem is truly Joseph's ancestral home, as Luke says, then there may well be some property in the town that once belonged to his family and to which he believes that he has a claim. We will examine such a possibility in greater detail as this book progresses. But Luke makes it quite clear that, if that family once owned any land there, it is now out of their control. The picture of the birth of Jesus that Luke is offering is one of him being born into complete poverty, not into the patrimony of a wealthy landowner.

We are left with no good explanation for the way in which Luke says this census was taken. This is particularly odd because Luke and all his earliest readers must have been familiar enough with the procedures for being registered in an imperial census. They must have been registered themselves at some point in their lives. So this would have been a puzzling element in the story from earliest times, but with time, distance and familiarity it came to be accepted without people asking the once obvious questions.

GALILEE IS NOT PART OF JUDEA

In this discussion, a great deal hinges on what particular census Luke is talking about and when it was taken. If he is indeed talking about the census taken under Quirinius in 6 CE, it creates yet another problem. That census *only* applied to Judea, Samaria and the rest of Syria Province. Galilee was not, at this date, an official part of the Roman world but rather a *tetrarchy* ruled by Herod the Great's son Herod Antipas on Rome's behalf. Since Herod Antipas was responsible for the administration of his territories, an imperial census would not be taken in Galilee.[13] It would seem that, even if the Romans did require the people of Judea to return to their ancestral homes to be registered (which seems doubtful), such a requirement would not have applied to Joseph in Nazareth of Galilee.

---

[13] Brown, p. 396.

Censuses and taxation were a matter for men. Except for in extraordinary circumstances, women did not own property or wealth, and so, normally, did not count when it came to the census takers. Even if some obscure reason could be found in Roman law or practice for Joseph to be obliged to make the journey from Nazareth to Bethlehem to be registered in the census, there is no reason why his wife (who, by the way, is not even his wife yet according to Luke, but merely his betrothed)[14] should be compelled to accompany him.

Why did Mary go with Joseph then? Luke does not even attempt to explain this. Surely, some arrangements could have been made for her to remain with friends or family when she was so close to the time to deliver her child. Why make such a risky journey (risky for herself and for her child) if she had no obligation to do so and if her presence meant nothing so far as the Romans were concerned?

WHAT DO WE DO WITH LUKE'S ACCOUNT?

There are, therefore, some substantial problems with Luke's account of the journey from Nazareth to Bethlehem and of the reasons for it. But I am not ready to abandon his story and conclude that it is untrustworthy and contains no truth. On the contrary, I find his account to be very truthful. But it is going to take some work to discover exactly where that truth lies.

We need to understand at the outset that modern people have very different standards for judging whether something is true or not than people did at the time this gospel was written. Modern people tend to judge the truthfulness of an historical account based on one question alone: did it all happen exactly as it says it happened? We look for accuracy in reporting all the details because we have been trained to do so by the modern methods and ethical codes of journalists and, to some extent, historians.

Ancient people didn't look at such questions in that way. They would have been far more interested in the *meaning* of something that happened than in getting all of the details reported exactly. So long as the account successfully conveyed the meaning of the event, they would have been happy enough to judge it to be true. Sometimes, in order to get the meaning across to people forcefully

---

[14] Luke 2:5

enough, they would not hesitate to change certain details in the account. This was particularly true of evangelists who were writing to convey important theological truth.

So, to begin with, it would be foolish for us to expect Luke's account to be absolutely correct in all its details—to describe everything exactly as it happened—because he likely did not understand that to be his job. He clearly wrote his gospel to convey the truth about Jesus. He wrote the nativity story, not simply to record all the things that took place around the birth of Jesus, but to proclaim what it meant that Jesus Christ came to earth and lived among us. We must never forget that this is what is most important to this gospel writer—not that he accurately present all of the historical data, but that he clearly present the meaning of the life of Jesus.

The odd thing about Luke's Gospel and one of the things that sets it apart from the others is that he seems to be very interested in the historical data. He often makes use of historical events to bring out the truths about Jesus or about his followers, and he is quite knowledgeable about such events. We see that in the nativity story. He knows about the initial census that really was taken in 6 CE, he is aware that Quirinius was governor of Syria around the time that Jesus was born, and we will see that he is aware of a great deal more than that.

I suspect that his interest in such events doesn't merely come from a desire to give an accurate portrayal of the political situation when Jesus was born. Luke is using these events to proclaim truths about Jesus.

Fortunately, in his writings, Luke gives us many opportunities to observe his methods of using and dealing with historical information. The Gospel of Luke is unique among all of the gospels in the Bible in that it is part of a two-volume work. Sometime after he finished writing the gospel, the same author decided to take up his pen again and continue the story in the book that we know as The Acts of the Apostles.

In the Acts we are often given the opportunity to see how Luke used the historical information that was available to him. Consider, for example, the following two passages—one taken from Luke's Acts of the Apostles and the other taken from the letters of Paul:

ACTS 9:19, 23-25

For several days [Saul] was with the disciples in Damascus... After some time had passed, the Jews

plotted to kill him, but their plot became known to
Saul. They were watching the gates day and night
so that they might kill him; but his disciples took
him by night and let him down through an opening
in the wall, lowering him in a basket.

2 CORINTHIANS 11:31-33

The God and Father of the Lord Jesus (blessed be
he forever!) knows that I do not lie. In Damascus,
the governor under King Aretas guarded the city of
Damascus in order to seize me, but I was let down
in a basket through a window in the wall, and
escaped from his hands.

These two passages are clearly describing the same historical
event—the escape of Paul (or Saul as he was known at the time)
from Damascus. They agree on the extraordinary manner of the
escape which makes it appear that Luke has access to some good
historical information as he writes.

But these two accounts of this same event also disagree with
one another about the reason why the escape was necessary.
According to Paul himself, he was escaping arrest by the king,
Aretas, and the local Roman governor. But according to Luke, Paul
had to flee from Damascus because the local Jewish community was
seeking to murder him.

It would be hard to doubt Paul's account of the events, given
that he was, after all, the man in the basket. He knew very well who
he was running away from and why. His account also seems more
plausible as it is unlikely that expatriate Jews would have had so
much influence in a Gentile city like Damascus. Luke has evidently
adjusted the facts of the story and it is not too hard to find his
reasons for doing so.

Throughout the Book of Acts, Luke always highlights the
Jewish opposition to the preaching of Paul. He often blames the
Jews for being the cause of any persecution or opposition. He puts
such an emphasis on this Jewish opposition, not only because it is
related to what happened (surely Paul did have many Jewish
enemies), but also because it is related to his theological
understanding of the ministry of Paul. Luke makes Jewish
opposition to the preaching of Paul a major theme of the Book of
Acts.

In addition, throughout the Book of Acts, Luke has a tendency
to play down any Roman opposition to the ministry of Paul. This is

likely because he is trying to avoid negative attention from the imperial authorities. He wants to present a church that is not dangerous to the empire in order to persuade the empire that it need not persecute the church. Luke naturally hesitates to admit that Roman authorities such as client kings and governors might have found fault with his main character, Paul of Tarsus. He would much rather deflect any blame for opposition to Paul onto local Jewish groups even though Paul clearly states in his letter to the Corinthians that he was in trouble with the local Roman authorities in Damascus.[15]

And so we see how Luke is willing to take genuine historical information that he has gleaned from his sources and use it, not simply to give an account of exactly what happened but, to develop an important theological theme and to make important points in defence of the church. If Luke was willing to do this in his accounts of the adventures of Paul, there is no reason to think that he wouldn't be willing to do much the same thing in his account of the birth of Jesus.

This is a very important point and I want to stress it. I believe that Luke is very knowledgeable about historical events and he often betrays that knowledge in his writings. To give another example, Luke knows about a certain Gallio who was a Roman official, called a proconsul, in the Province of Achaia. He recounts a trial of Paul in Corinth, the capital of Achaia, before this official in his Book of Acts.[16] We know very well that Luke is correct about the identity of Gallio because an inscription has been found dating his proconsulship. "We are certain Gallio was in Corinth for the summer and early fall of either 51 or 52 C.E."[17] It is rather extraordinary that Luke, writing decades later, should know about the relatively short tenure of this official and that he should so definitely place Paul there at that time.

Although Luke is knowledgeable about political events in Achaia at that time, that does not necessarily mean that we can always trust him to use his knowledge in a simple and straightforward manner. His mention of Gallio indicates that he is saying that Paul did not arrive in Corinth—and therefore did not enter Europe for the first time—until about 50 CE.[18] That would put

---

[15] These themes are explored at great length in John Dominic Crossan and Jonathan L. Reed, *In Search of Paul*, HarperSanFrancisco, 2004.

[16] Acts 18:12 -17

[17] Crossan and Reed, p. 34.

[18] Acts 16:9-12

Paul's European mission—a significant part of what he called his "task of preaching the gospel to the Gentiles"[19]—very late in his career. It would push the bulk of Paul's preaching ministry into the last decade of his life. This has led many to doubt Luke's chronology of Paul's presence in Corinth and to suggest that he must have been there, for the first time at least, earlier than that.[20] So, while Luke's knowledge of the history seems to be excellent, his particular chronology for Paul's journey is somewhat doubtful.

As long as we keep in mind that Luke is far more interested in making his theological points than he is in relating the simple sequence of events, we can understand why he depicts the chronology in this way. As he announces at the beginning of the Book of Acts, he is seeking to portray an orderly theological progression of the gospel as it is preached "in Jerusalem, in all Judea and Samaria, and to the ends of the earth."[21] This sense of order is so important to Luke that he feels that Paul's ministry in Europe must wait until Paul is given a specific mandate to preach to the Gentiles by the leaders of the church in Jerusalem which only happens relatively late at a council in Jerusalem that Luke describes in Acts 15:1-35. That is why he uses his historical knowledge to portray Paul's entry into Europe so late.

Although Luke knows the history fairly well, therefore, he is just more interested in using his knowledge to make his theological points than he is in constructing a strictly correct narrative. This is something we must remember about Luke as we continue to read his accounts. Often it will only be when we understand the theological point he is trying to make that we are able to appreciate how he is using his historical data.

For this reason, I believe that it is possible for us to find and embrace the truth in Luke's nativity story. But to do that we need to understand better what Luke is doing with his historical information—how he is using it, what points he is trying to make and what theological themes he is supporting with it. That is why I am convinced that a closer look at Luke's birth narrative may help us to clear up many of these difficulties. In order to do that, however, we must first try to answer some primary questions:

- Given that we have two separate and independent accounts of Jesus's birth in the New Testament, Matthew's and

---

[19] Galatians 2:7

[20] See Garry Wills, *What Paul Meant*, Viking, 2006. pp. 151-155

[21] Acts 1:8

Luke's, to what extent can we or should we attempt to harmonize these two accounts?

- Luke clearly attempts to be very clear in his dating of certain events in his Gospel. When, exactly, does he consider that Jesus was born and how does he use this historical setting to present theological truths?

- New Testament writers—especially Evangelists—used the Old Testament as a major source for their writing, often using the stories of Biblical heroes to fill in any blanks they had in their sources. What are the Old Testament passages that Luke is drawing on as he writes his birth narrative?

Once we have answered these questions, we can begin to explore Luke's birth narrative and understand how he is using it to give a true account of Jesus's birth, according to the standards of truth for his time.

INTERLUDE: THE REGION BETWEEN SAMARIA AND GALILEE

As the couple travels, they pass over some very different terrains on their way to Judea and to Bethlehem. Eventually they come to the region between Samaria and Galilee—a cultural no man's land.

It is not that uncommon for Jews in Galilee to travel to Judea—most often because they are going to Jerusalem to take part in various religious festivals. However, few Jews take the most direct route because it leads through Samaria. Jews and Samaritans do not get along. They disagree in too many matters of faith and religion.

So, as they approach the border of Samaria, Joseph and Mary naturally turn toward the Jordan River. They will cross the river and pass by Samaria on the east. For several miles, they have the opportunity to walk along the border between Antipas's territory in the north and the new Roman province in the south. They are shocked by how much the region has recently changed.

In the days of King Herod, Galilee, Samaria and Judea had all been united under one ruler and, although Herod had hardly been popular, that had at least made travel a bit easier.

Since Herod's death things have been very different. First the kingdom was divided between his sons—Archelaus in the south and Antipas in the north. For about a decade, the two highly competitive brothers have taken great pleasure collecting hefty tolls from travellers crossing the new frontier in both directions.

But now that the Romans have tired of Archelaus's rule in Judea and Samaria, they have removed him and taken direct control of that region. Things are now very different in the south.

Nowhere is the new state of affairs as clear as on the border between Galilee and Samaria. For a long time Herod's family effectively masked Roman power in Judea and Samaria even if it had always been there behind the scenes. There is no longer any attempt to hide it. Everywhere you look you are reminded of the emperor's authority and the consequences of disobedience. It is particularly true at the border, especially right now when there is a large contingent of Roman troops as well as many toll collectors.

The soldiers seem to be on edge. Their weapons are always close at hand and they move about in large contingents. Joseph begins to suspect that this has to do with more than just preparations for a census or with an unusual number of travellers in the area. They seem to be afraid.

Soon the couple begins to overhear excited talk from other travellers. There are rumours of raids against Roman outposts and patrols. There has been no violence, but supplies have been stolen and communications and supply lines have been disrupted. No one has seen anything firsthand, but everyone seems to be talking about it. It certainly seems to explain the mood that Joseph sees among the troops. The first response they have to anything that seems threatening is to increase the level of violence and oppression.

Every few miles they have to pass through another checkpoint. As Mary and Joseph approach the next one, a young soldier looks up. He scans them warily, looking for any signs of insubordination and checking for hidden weapons.

"Where are you going," the soldier asks in Greek. A slave hovers nearby and quickly translates the question into Joseph's native tongue of Aramaic.[22] No one asks

---

[22] We do not know how the Roman army communicated with the foreign people whose territories they occupied. It seems unlikely that they would have bothered to learn the local languages in every territory. Slaves were plentiful and many spoke both Greek and the local languages. They

anything of Mary. Anything she might have to say doesn't matter.

"We're going to Bethlehem in Judea," Joseph replies. "We are on a holy pilgrimage."

"Another festival? You people seem to have them every other week!"

"Yeah," says Joseph sullenly, "something like that."

They are asked many other questions—where they have come from, how they feel about Antipas and the Emperor. They answer in such a way as to make their loyalty to their rulers seem genuine although the soldier clearly does not believe them. Everything they are carrying is thoroughly searched but, fortunately, they have nothing that a Roman would consider worth stealing.

They are delayed for many hours with meaningless requirements. This is what often happens. Those who can afford it usually offer a bribe to be able to move along more quickly, but that is hardly an option for the couple from Nazareth. They are patient because they have no choice. They put up with the inconvenience and discomfort and they wait. Ultimately, they waste a full day at the checkpoint and they know that there will be several more to pass in the miles ahead. But as the sun goes down they are finally given permission to pass and they continue on their way, one stage closer to Bethlehem.

---

may have been purchased or rented as translators when necessary. Although Latin was becoming a kind of lingua franca in the western empire in the first century, legionaries in the eastern empire would have learned to function in Hellenistic Greek which had been used ever since the time of Alexander the Great as the language of government, administration and trade throughout the region.

2) SHOULD THE TWO BIRTH ACCOUNTS BE HARMONIZED?

The Gospel of Luke and the Gospel of Matthew have a great deal in common. They share much of the same material on the life and sayings of Jesus though they organize it somewhat differently. As far as we can understand from a study of the two texts, both Gospels were written independently (with neither making any reference to, nor apparently even having any knowledge of, the other) towards the end of the first century CE or perhaps even later.

Both gospels were written anonymously—with no names attached. It didn't take the church very long to decide that they must have been written respectively by Matthew, one of Jesus's twelve apostles, and Luke, an associate of Paul. But that is just tradition. The truth of the matter is that we really have no idea who might have written these books. All we have to help us to understand the interests, concerns and theological agendas of these two authors is what we find in the words they wrote, and it is better not to read anything into what they have written based on church tradition. I will continue to refer to these authors using the names that tradition gave them for the sake of convenience, but please keep in mind that the Matthew and Luke I am talking about are, in fact, figures of mystery whose true identities we may never know.

A deep study of the two gospels has led to a significant scholarly consensus that they shared common literary sources for much of their material. In particular, the theory has been put forward and generally accepted that they both used the Gospel of Mark (or perhaps an early version of it) as a source and that they also shared another major source that no longer exists apart from its traces in these two gospels. This other theoretical source is commonly called the "Q Gospel."[23]

Because of these shared sources, parallels abound in the texts of these two gospels. But the birth narratives are quite different. Only these two authors attempted any sort of account of the birth of Jesus. (Of course, there are other non-canonical accounts of the birth of Jesus, such as *The Infancy Gospel of James*, but they were written later and were undoubtedly dependant on these two

---

[23] Many books have been written on the "Two source hypothesis." There is an excellent summary of the theory in Christopher Tuckett, *Methods of Interpretation*, Fortress Press, Philadelphia, 1987. pp.78-94.

gospels.)[24] When Matthew and Luke came to write their gospels, their primary source materials likely made no more than passing references to the birth of Jesus, if they said anything at all. Both of them felt the need to include a story of the birth of Jesus anyway.

This would have made perfect sense to them. They naturally assumed that anyone as extraordinary as Jesus who had done and said such remarkable things and who had sparked such a powerful movement must have had an extraordinary birth. This was a common way of thinking in the ancient world. Once individuals, such as Alexander the Great, Julius Caesar and Caesar Augustus, rose to great prominence, people naturally began to think and speculate on the extraordinary conceptions and births that they must have had.

But a fascination with Jesus's birth must have developed relatively late. In fact, it doesn't seem to have been a point of interest at all in the earliest Christians writings such as the letters of the Apostle Paul. The Gospel of Mark also says nothing about it. So when Matthew and Luke began their accounts of the nativity, they could only draw from very sketchy source material at best. This seems evident from the fact that they actually only agree on a few select details in their narratives while they actually differ substantially in other matters.

POINTS OF AGREEMENT

There are three main points of agreement between the two stories: the *location* of Jesus's birth, the *names* of his parents and the *virginal state* of his mother.

PLACE OF BIRTH

Both gospels agree that Jesus was born at Bethlehem in Judea. This is actually quite extraordinary given that, when they were written, anyone who knew anything about Jesus knew that he was actually from the village of Nazareth in far distant Galilee. The other gospels and earliest Christian writings betray no knowledge that Jesus was from Bethlehem. The Gospel of John even makes a point of insisting on Jesus's origins from Nazareth despite the fact that this appears to be a very negative thing:

[24] R. J. Miller, Ed. *The Complete Gospels*, Annotated Scholars Version, HarperSanFrancisco, 1994. pp. 380-382

Philip found Nathanael and said to him, "We have found him about whom Moses in the law and also the prophets wrote, Jesus son of Joseph from Nazareth." Nathanael said to him, "Can anything good come out of Nazareth?"[25]

Later on, this same gospel records a significant controversy over Jesus's origins from Galilee:

When they heard these words, some in the crowd said, "This is really the prophet." Others said, "This is the Messiah." But some asked, "Surely the Messiah does not come from Galilee, does he? Has not the scripture said that the Messiah is descended from David and comes from Bethlehem, the village where David lived?" So there was a division in the crowd because of him. Some of them wanted to arrest him, but no one laid hands on him.[26]

As it recounts such stories, the Gospel of John has a perfect opportunity to address the readers directly (as it does in other places)[27] and explain that, though Jesus grew up in Nazareth, he had actually been born in Bethlehem, which would surely answer both Nathaniel's and the crowd's objections to Jesus. The fact that it does not do so is a strong indication that any story about a birth in Bethlehem was not well known, if known at all, in the early church. Or it could even mean that, if there was such a tradition and John was aware of it, he was actively disputing its accuracy.

So it is rather interesting that both Matthew and Luke seem to have independently come to believe that Jesus was born in Bethlehem. Nevertheless, it is really not very hard to explain how that could have happened. There is a very clear Old Testament prophecy (explicitly cited in Matthew 2:6 and likely also in mind in the above passage from the Gospel of John) which had created an expectation in some quarters that the Messiah, when he came, would come from Bethlehem because it was the city where King David had been born:

But you, O Bethlehem of Ephrathah,
who are one of the little clans of Judah,
from you shall come forth for me

---

[25] John 1:45-46
[26] John 7:40-44. See also John 7:52.
[27] John 19:35

one who is to rule in Israel,
whose origin is from of old,
from ancient days.[28]

Because of this clear prophecy, it is quite likely that both evangelists would have believed that Jesus *must* have come from Bethlehem whether or not they had any evidence that he had been born there. This agreement is easily explained, therefore, despite the fact that there is no indication that either evangelist had any reference to a birth in Bethlehem in his source material.

PARENTS

Matthew and Luke also agree on the identity of Jesus's parents: Mary and Joseph. They would have had Mary's name from their common source, the Gospel of Mark, where she is named, along with Jesus's brothers but, strangely, without any mention of a father:

> On the sabbath he began to teach in the synagogue, and many who heard him were astounded. They said, "Where did this man get all this? What is this wisdom that has been given to him? What deeds of power are being done by his hands! Is not this the carpenter, the son of Mary and brother of James and Joses and Judas and Simon, and are not his sisters here with us?" And they took offense at him.[29]

So it is not at all surprising that the two evangelists should agree on the name of Jesus's mother, but their agreement on the name of the father is a little harder to explain since he is not mentioned in Mark and likely not in the Q Gospel either. I would suggest that these two Gospel writers shared another source or tradition that identified Jesus's father as Joseph. This does not seem unlikely because, even though Mark does not name a father, the Gospel of John, which was likely written somewhat later than Matthew and Luke, but that also used some of its own separate source material, does give Jesus's name as "Jesus son of Joseph from Nazareth."[30]

---

[28] Micah 5:2
[29] Mark 6:2-3
[30] John 1:45

In the Gospel of Matthew, it is made abundantly clear that Mary was a virgin when Jesus was conceived and that she continued in that state until she gave birth to him. The Lucan story seems to affirm the same thing, though not so clearly. J. A. Fitzmyer has argued that, "When [Luke's] account is read in and for itself—without the overtones of the Matthean annunciation to Joseph—every detail of it could be understood of a child to be born to Mary in the usual way."[31] But most scholars who have looked at the question have come to the conclusion that the underlying assumption of a virginal conception is there in Luke as well.[32]

So I would not hesitate to say that Matthew and Luke agree on the virginity of Mary. This is a remarkable agreement because it is an idea that is unlikely to have come from their primary source material. It is not even a question that comes up in the Gospel of Mark unless it is a concern that could be read into Mark's failure to name a father for Jesus, which seems unlikely. And, unlike the matter of the Messiah being born in Bethlehem, there is no clear Old Testament prophecy that requires that the Messiah be born of a virgin.

Matthew relates the virgin birth to a passage from the prophet Isaiah (which he cites in the Septuagint translation that contains the keyword *virgin*):

> All this took place to fulfill what had been spoken
> by the Lord through the prophet:
>> "Look, the virgin shall conceive and bear a son,
>> and they shall name him Emmanuel,"
> which means, "God is with us."[33]

Matthew uses this passage to explain why Jesus had to be born of a virgin—because it had been prophesied. It helps him to come to a deeper understanding of the meaning of the incarnation of the Christ which he sees as a way in which "God is with us."

Many would argue today that Matthew has misinterpreted that prophecy in Isaiah by taking it out of context and relying on a defective Greek translation. They would suggest that, in the context

---

[31] Fitzmyer, J.A., "The Virginal Conception of Jesus in the New Testament," *Theological Studies*, 34 (1973) pp. 566-67.

[32] Raymond Brown devotes a great deal of time examining this argument and comes to the conclusion that Luke is in fact clearly saying that Mary remained a virgin until Jesus was born. Brown, pp. 298-309.

[33] Matthew 2:22,23; quoting the Greek Septuagint of Isaiah 7:14

of the original passage in the original language, the prophet was actually speaking about a child that would be born to a young woman in the king's household in his own day. But that matters little to Matthew, who obviously believes that much of what he reads in the Old Testament refers directly to the life and acts of Jesus.

Luke, when he grapples with the meaning of the virgin birth, doesn't seem to have the Isaiah passage in mind at all. He certainly doesn't mention it. He seems to be drawing rather on the stories from Genesis of Abraham and Sarah and their struggle to conceive a child despite Sarah's infertility. When Mary is told by the angel Gabriel that she will conceive, her reaction is to say, "How will this be… since I am a virgin?"[34] Her response is reminiscent of the response of Sarah who is told in the Book of Genesis that she will conceive and have a child despite the fact that she is very old and post-menopausal.[35] Sarah also expresses incredulity in the face of a prediction of a conception that seems impossible, although the particular reason for the impossibility in her case is quite different.

Luke also seeks inspiration from the story of Hannah, the mother of the prophet Samuel—another woman who struggled to conceive a child. Mary's song that celebrates her expectation of the birth of her son has many parallels to the song of Hannah:

THE SONG OF HANNAH

> "My heart exults in the LORD;
> my strength is exalted in my God.
> My mouth derides my enemies,
> because I rejoice in my victory.
> The bows of the mighty are broken,
> but the feeble gird on strength.
> Those who were full have hired themselves out for bread,
> but those who were hungry are fat with spoil.
> The barren has borne seven,
> but she who has many children is forlorn.
> The LORD kills and brings to life;
> he brings down to Sheol and raises up.
> The LORD makes poor and makes rich;
> he brings low, he also exalts.
> He raises up the poor from the dust;

---

[34] Luke 1:34
[35] e.g. Genesis 15:1-6, 18:9-15

he lifts the needy from the ash heap,
to make them sit with princes
and inherit a seat of honour."[36]

"My soul magnifies the Lord,
and my spirit rejoices in God my Saviour,
for he has looked with favour on the lowliness of
his servant.
Surely, from now on all generations will call me
blessed;
for the Mighty One has done great things for me,
and holy is his name.
His mercy is for those who fear him
from generation to generation.
He has shown strength with his arm;
he has scattered the proud in the thoughts of their
hearts.
He has brought down the powerful from their
thrones,
and lifted up the lowly;
he has filled the hungry with good things,
and sent the rich away empty."[37]

Luke is clearly trying to come to grips with the unexpected and improbable pregnancy of Mary and he does so by reflecting on the unexpected and improbable pregnancies of women like Sarah and Hannah in the Old Testament. Of course, Mary's case is unique because the reason why her pregnancy is unexpected is quite different from the reasons why Sarah and Hannah were not expected to have children. Sarah shouldn't have had a child because she was too old, Hannah, because she was infertile, while Mary should not have become pregnant because she was a virgin. The reasons are different but there is a common theme of miraculous conception that runs through all three stories. Luke must have seen enough similarities between these three women to convince him that these Old Testament stories had been placed there to help him to explain a virgin birth.

So the two evangelists turn to very different Old Testament scriptures to understand the virginity of Mary and what it means.

---

[36] 1 Samuel 2:1, 4-8
[37] Luke 1:46-53

This suggests to me that they each have a puzzling piece of information that they are trying to understand. That is to say that they both have a piece of tradition—a teaching that has been passed down to them from the earlier church—that indicates that Jesus was born of a virgin and they are trying to comprehend it.

The New Testament writers often turned to important Old Testament stories to help them process and understand the things that happened to Jesus, and that is what Matthew and Luke do here. But they turn to quite different places: Matthew turns to the Prophet Isaiah while Luke turns to the Book of Genesis and to 1 Samuel.

That is why I think that Matthew and Luke are indeed drawing on an established early Christian tradition regarding the virginity of Mary. This point of agreement is very significant because it indicates that the church (or at least certain parts of it) very early on accepted a view of the conception and birth of Jesus that would have been really quite shocking to Jewish sensibilities. Although the notion of gods fathering children on human mothers was quite common in Greek myths and legends, the Jews had never told such stories about their God.

POINTS OF DISAGREEMENT

In effect, we have three primary points on which these two evangelists agree. Obviously, these agreements are very important and meaningful, but we should not ignore the points on which they diverge. Unfortunately, these differences are not all that easy for us to see because we are in the habit of harmonizing these two accounts. Christian tradition has, for almost two thousand years, easily integrated the two birth narratives to the point that, when we think of the nativity, we automatically place Mary, Joseph and the baby at the manger surrounded by angels and shepherds (all elements from Luke's story). We also add the Magi approaching with their gifts and the star shining overhead (from Matthew's gospel). When we forget all those centuries of tradition and simply read Matthew's gospel as if we'd never heard of anything that happens in Luke's, and vice versa, we realize just how different these two stories really are. I see ten major points of divergence.

1. HOW THE COUPLE CAME TO BE IN BETHLEHEM

Both Matthew and Luke were faced with a problem as they wrote their birth narratives. They knew very well that Jesus was from Nazareth in Galilee. Anyone who knew anything about Jesus knew that. But they also knew that, if he was the Messiah, he had to be from Bethlehem just like it said in the Book of Micah. So they each had to explain how Jesus of Nazareth came to be born in far off Bethlehem. Both evangelists were able to deal with this problem, but they dealt with it in very different ways.

Luke's solution we have already discussed. Luke says that Mary and Joseph were originally from Nazareth, he calls it "their own town,"[38] and explains that they just happened to be in Bethlehem temporarily at the time of Jesus's birth because they had travelled there to register during the census.

Matthew's solution is quite different. If you simply forget everything that you have ever read in the Gospel of Luke (not to mention every Christmas pageant you have ever seen) and read Matthew's story at face value, it is quite clear that he is operating under the assumption that both Mary and Joseph are from Bethlehem. It is their home town and they even have a house there that they share once they are married and where the Magi visit them: "On entering *the house*, they saw the child with Mary his mother; and they knelt down and paid him homage."[39]

Matthew has the opposite problem of Luke. He must explain why this couple who are from Bethlehem end up raising Jesus in the little village of Nazareth. This he does very handily in the following passage:

> When Herod died, an angel of the Lord suddenly
> appeared in a dream to Joseph in Egypt and said,
> "Get up, take the child and his mother, and go to
> the land of Israel, for those who were seeking the
> child's life are dead." Then Joseph got up, took the
> child and his mother, and went to the land of
> Israel. But when he heard that Archelaus was ruling
> over Judea in place of his father Herod, he was
> afraid to go there. And after being warned in a
> dream, he went away to the district of
> Galilee. There he made his home in a town called
> Nazareth, so that what had been spoken through
> the prophets might be fulfilled, "He will be called a
> Nazorean."[40]

---

[38] Luke 2:39
[39] Matthew 2:11. Emphasis added.
[40] Matthew 2:19-23

As far as Matthew is concerned, Joseph isn't from Nazareth at all. He only ends up there because it seems to be a good place to escape the notice of Archelaus, and because it was required in order to fulfill a prophecy. Matthew fails to explain why the family would have been safer under the jurisdiction of Herod Antipas, who was also a son of Herod the Great, in Galilee, and so his explanation is far from ideal.

One gospel writer says that Mary and Joseph were from Nazareth and just happened to be staying temporarily in Bethlehem when Jesus was born while the other assumes they were from Bethlehem and only raised Jesus in Nazareth to establish a new life away from one of Herod's sons. This is the first and greatest contradiction between the two nativity stories and it cannot be easily overcome. There are many more.

2. GENEALOGY

Both Matthew and Luke give a list of the ancestors of Jesus. Matthew traces his lineage back to Abraham and Luke goes all the way back to Adam. They agree on the very important point that, as Messiah, Jesus is a direct descendant of King David. This information was found in their source material. The Gospel of Mark refers to Jesus as the "son of David."[41] In addition, there seems to have been a very clear expectation among many Jews, based on Old Testament prophecy, that the Messiah, when he came, would be a descendant of David in some sense.[42]

Although they both make this all-important connection between Jesus and David in their genealogies, they do it through different ancestors. The genealogies do not correspond at all through several generations. Here is how the two accounts differ in the crucial generations:

LINE OF DESCENT ACCORDING TO MATTHEW 1:6-16:

David, Solomon, Rehoboam, Abijah, Asaph,
Jehoshaphat, Joram, Uzziah, Jotham, Ahaz,
Hezekiah, Manasseh, Amos, Josiah, Jechoniah,
Salathiel, Zerubbabel, Abiud, Eliakim, Azor,
Zadok, Achim, Eliud, Eleazar, Matthan, Jacob,
Joseph, Jesus

---

[41] Mark 10:37 and 12:45, although the latter is somewhat ambiguous.
[42] Jeremiah 23:5-6

> **David**, Nathan, Mattatha, Menna, Melea, Eliakim,
> Jonam, Joseph, Judah, Simeon, Levi, Matthat,
> Jorim, Eliezer, Joshua, Er, Elmadam, Cosam, Addi,
> Melchi, Neri, Shealtiel, Zerubbabel, Rhesa, Joanan,
> Joda, Josech, Semein, Mattathias, Maath, Naggai,
> Esli, Nahum, Amos, Mattathias, Joseph, Jannai,
> Melchi, Levi, Matthat, Heli, **Joseph, Jesus**

The lists are so glaringly different that the contradictions cannot be ignored. Down through many centuries, therefore, attempts have been made at harmonizing the two genealogies. The most popular solution is to say that one gospel (usually Matthew) is giving the ancestors of Joseph while the other (usually Luke) is giving those of Mary.[43] It is not, however, a very plausible explanation. Ancient Mediterranean society was extremely patrilineal—tracing descent exclusively through males—so it seems very unlikely that either gospel writer would have departed from the normal manner of recording a genealogy without clearly indicating what he was doing.

Arguments have been made that, when Luke writes, "[Jesus] was the son (as was thought) of Joseph son of Heli,"[44] what he actually means is "Joseph was the *son in law* of Heli" or, "Jesus was *supposedly* the son of Joseph but actually the grandson of Heli," but neither of these translations is grammatically possible.[45]

It is also worth noting that at no point in his gospel does Luke suggest that Mary was a descendant of David. It is Joseph who is "descended from the house and family of David."[46] In fact, Luke even suggests that Mary is connected to a different tribe from David, who came from the tribe of Judah. At least, he says that Mary was a close relative of Elizabeth who was "a descendant of Aaron" in the tribe of Levi.[47] It seems rather unlikely, therefore, that Luke thought that Mary was a descendant of David.

A more complex solution is to propose that the two genealogies are different because one traces direct descent while the other traces descent through adoption as was sometimes required by Hebrew law, particularly the law of levirate marriage.[48] This theory has found

---

[43] A solution first proposed by Annius of Viterbo in 1490 CE. See I. Howard Marshall, p.158.

[44] Luke 3:23

[45] I. Howard Marshall, p. 158. Raymond E. Brown, p. 89.

[46] Luke 2:3

[47] Luke 1:8, 1:36.

little support in modern times.[49] The most popular modern theory is to say that "Matthew gives the legal line of descent from David, stating who was the heir to the throne in each case, but Luke gives the actual descendants of David in the branch of the family to which Joseph belonged."[50] This really solves little because it still leaves us with two contradictory lists that cannot be reconciled. This indicates that, if Matthew and Luke have any literary record at all beyond Old Testament genealogies, they have two different and completely contradictory lists. Any attempt to harmonize the two will be a futile exercise.

There are more significant differences between these two genealogies than just the contradictions between specific names. The two lists are very different in terms of underlying meaning as well. The list that Matthew offers includes not only King David but also many of his royal descendants who also ruled over the Kingdom of Judah.[51] With such a list, he is making the point that Jesus is the heir to the entire royal line of Judah, not just to David. This is probably a part of Matthew's overall effort to emphasise the kingliness of Jesus throughout his gospel.

But Luke's genealogy names no kings other than David. This gives his list a different tone. He seems to be recounting the history of a very different family—a fairly normal Jewish family that just happens to have one very illustrious ancestor. I suspect that Luke is thinking of Joseph as belonging to a less successful branch of David's family. They were not the ones who went onto great things but rather the ones who stayed behind in Bethlehem and continued to live on and farm the land that they inherited from Jesse, David's father.

This would also be the same land that is featured in the Book of Ruth—the land on which Ruth gleans during harvest time and where she meets her future husband, Boaz, whom Luke lists as the great grandfather of King David.[52] The family that Luke is thinking of may have lived on this famous piece of land but he still sees them as the poor rural cousins of the powerful kings who ruled in

---

[48] See Deuteronomy 25:5-10, Luke 20:28.

[49] I. Howard Marshall, p. 158.

[50] Ibid.

[51] See 1 Chronicles 3:10-16. All of the names between David and Jechoniah are no doubt intended to be the names of kings who ruled in Jerusalem. Spelling variations between the Old Testament names and the names that appear in Matthew are there because Matthew is writing in Greek, not Hebrew.

[52] Ruth 2,3,4; Luke 3:31,32

Jerusalem—forgotten and left in obscurity for generations until that line of kings had failed and their time finally came.

So, with his genealogy, Luke places the emphasis on Jesus's humble origins—an emphasis that certainly fits with his presentation of Jesus as a humble man, friend of the poor and lowly.

---

3. THE POLITICAL CLIMATE

As we have already noted, in Matthew's Gospel, the political shadow of Herod the Great looms large. He seems to have absolute power of life and death over all the people. In Luke's gospel, Herod has no influence over events at all and the only power we hear of is the power of Rome.

---

4. DATE

There is, I suggest, a contradiction in dating. This is a very controversial point of difference and I will look more deeply into this question in a future chapter, but I will simply posit for now that a simple, straightforward reading of each gospel without reference to the other will lead to the conclusion that they are saying that Jesus was born at a different time. The difference is about a decade.

---

5. SOCIO-ECONOMIC STATUS

In Luke's narrative, Jesus is famously born into abject poverty and laid in a manger because of a lack of adequate housing. The idea seems to be that this poverty is temporary and is a result of the extraordinary travelling associated with the census. Nevertheless, the lowly social position of Jesus at his birth has important symbolic meaning to the author of this gospel and introduces a theme that will be developed through the rest of his story of Jesus's life and ministry.

Matthew makes no mention of such poverty. On the contrary, the family lives in a house in Bethlehem and they receive precious gifts of gold, frankincense and myrrh from the magi. They have sufficient wealth (perhaps because of the gifts) to make a sudden trip to Egypt and when they return from there they have enough financial independence to make their home in Nazareth, a place of their own choosing.

In Luke's Gospel, the news of the imminent birth of the Messiah is given exclusively to Mary by an angel who appears to her while she is awake.[53] In the Gospel of Matthew it is Joseph who receives the announcement from an angel in a dream.[54] There is, in this, a minor point of agreement, the annunciation of the birth by an angel. This agreement, together with certain similarities in the angelic message between the two gospels, has led Raymond Brown to suggest that there was a "basic pre-gospel annunciation tradition that each evangelist used in his own way."[55] Brown is saying that he thinks there was a tradition circulating in the early church that the birth of Jesus had been announced beforehand by an angel and that Luke and Matthew both heard it independently and incorporated it into their stories in different ways.

This is a very intriguing idea. But it does not change the fact that the two annunciation stories, as we have them, are very different. Not only is the announcement made to two different people, but it is also made at two significantly different times. According to Luke, Mary receives the news before she has even conceived the child while Matthew says that Joseph receives the news much later when the pregnancy has progressed enough to cause a public scandal and yet Joseph has apparently not heard anything from Mary or her family about the announcement that, according to Luke, had been made to Mary months earlier.[56]

This dissimilarity between the two gospels is more than just a matter of who was told what by whom and when. It marks a major difference between how these two writers are telling their story. In his account, Matthew makes Joseph his central character. Joseph is not just the one who receives the messages but also the one who takes all of the initiative. He decides to take Mary as his wife, he takes the family to Egypt and he is the one who decides that they should settle in Nazareth after the death of Herod the Great. Mary, for her part, says nothing and does nothing in Matthew's account apart from being pregnant and bearing a child. Joseph is the one who understands what is going on and who acts accordingly.

All of this is fairly turned around in the Gospel of Luke where the story is much more focussed on Mary, her feelings and her decisions. She is the one who chooses to submit to God's plan for

---

[53] Luke 1:26ff
[54] Matthew 1:20
[55] Brown, p. 159
[56] Matthew 1:18,19

her by saying, "Here am I, the servant of the Lord; let it be with me according to your word."[57] She is the one who treasures all that is said and attends to what happens and she ponders all of it in her heart.[58]

Joseph, in the Gospel of Luke, says nothing and does nothing except go up from Nazareth to Bethlehem because he belongs to the house and lineage of David. There is no indication at all in Luke's account that Joseph even knows what is going on. You might well expect, given the extraordinary means by which Luke says that Mary conceived her child, that Joseph should at least ask a few questions or lodge a few complaints, but, if he did, Luke certainly shows no interest in his concerns.

And so the existence of these two very different annunciation stories underlines the very different approaches that Matthew and Luke have taken to their accounts.

---

7. MARITAL STATUS

In both Gospels, Mary and Joseph are first introduced as two people who are engaged to be married. According to Matthew's account, the engagement lasts until the point when Mary's pregnancy begins to show which in turn creates something of a public scandal.[59] At this point, upon receiving a message from God in a dream, Joseph takes her as his wife, but has no marital relations with her until she has borne a son.[60] It would appear that Matthew is saying the couple were married at least a few months before the birth.

Luke tells the story a little bit differently. He introduces Mary initially as "a virgin engaged to a man whose name was Joseph."[61] And then, approximately nine months later, just before the birth of Jesus, he again refers to the couple not as married but as still engaged to be married: "He went to be registered with Mary, *to whom he was engaged* and who was expecting a child."[62] Luke gives no indication at all of when Mary and Joseph might have been married, but he strongly implies that it was not until after Jesus was born.

This does seem to be a contradiction, though, perhaps, we need not make too much of it. It seems likely that in first century

---

[57] Luke 1:38
[58] Luke 2:19
[59] Matthew 1:18
[60] Matthew 1:24-25
[61] Luke 1:27
[62] Luke 2:5, emphasis added.

Palestine the line between engagement and marriage could be somewhat blurry at times. The engagement was likely the more serious of the two as it was the moment when pledges were given and promises made. An engagement, once established, could not be broken without it being considered a divorce, as Matthew indicates in his account of Joseph's moral dilemma.[63] The marriage itself was more of an opportunity to celebrate the fact of the wife taking up residence in her husband's home and the physical consummation of the union as is evidenced in a number of Jesus's parables and sayings.[64] It is why both evangelists put the emphasis on the couple's engagement rather than on the marriage.

It would seem that neither evangelist is overly concerned with the date of the wedding. They are far more concerned with making it quite clear that there were no sexual relations between Mary and Joseph prior to the birth of Jesus because this is, for them, the essential theological point in the account. In fact, they both agree that the couple is betrothed and yet has not consummated its relationship. Luke works under the straightforward assumption that a betrothal that is not yet consummated is not yet a marriage, while Matthew finds it possible for the couple to be married and yet to have no marital relations. So, in effect, they are both saying the same thing but using different words because each has a different understanding of what marriage means and where the line between betrothal and marriage is drawn.

Therefore the differing descriptions of Mary and Joseph's marital status do not necessarily constitute a contradiction between the two gospel accounts. This is a case where they could both be correct according to their own definitions. The confusion does seem to indicate, nevertheless, that there was no established tradition about the marital status of this couple when these evangelists came to write their accounts.

8. ANGELS, DREAMS AND STARS

In both gospels the birth of Jesus is accompanied by heavenly messages. But the mode of communication differs sharply. Luke tells of angels who deliver their messages directly to Mary and, later, to a group shepherds. Communication from God always comes directly by means of these heavenly messengers.

---

[63] Matthew 1:19
[64] E.g. Matthew 25:1-13

In Matthew's Gospel, however, God communicates only through dreams. Twice an angel appears to Joseph in a dream, and once the Magi receive a message in a dream.[65] This difference in modes of communication is surely not insignificant. There is a very big difference between a message received while you are awake and fully aware and a message received in your sleep. For one thing, dreams always require interpretation in the Biblical tradition which would seem to make them a less certain way of communicating.[66] That Matthew only speaks of one type of communication while Luke only speaks of the other indicates that they are approaching the event of the birth from quite different angles.

In Matthew's Gospel, God also communicates, though even more indirectly, through the appearance of a star. This heavenly sign, however, must also be interpreted much like a dream and apparently only the Magi are able to discern the meaning in its appearance (though, of course, the magi inadvertently pass the information on to King Herod with tragic results). The star, despite our continued insistence on placing it above the manger, does not appear and is not mentioned in Luke's Gospel.

9. STATUS OF THE VISITORS

We certainly have two very different groups of people visiting the child Jesus in the two gospels. On the one hand, in Luke's Gospel, we have poor shepherds. Shepherds were considered to be on the very lowest rung of society. They were dirty, unkempt and generally shunned by the rest of society. Their attendance at the manger soon after the birth certainly adds to the humbleness of the family's circumstances and helps Luke to make clear the lowliness of the birth of the messiah.

In the Gospel of Matthew, on the other hand, the only visitors to the child who are mentioned are wise and learned Magi from a distant country. They must also be extremely wealthy men to be able to make such a long journey in response to a sign they have seen in the sky. Whatever point Matthew is trying to make by mentioning these visitors, it is certainly a very different one than Luke is making by talking about the shepherds.

---

[65] Matthew 1:20; 2:13; 2:12.
[66] Genesis 40:1-41:36; Daniel 2:1-45.

Both Matthew and Luke make a large number of both direct and indirect Biblical references in their accounts of Jesus's birth. Matthew tends to make the references quite overtly while Luke can be much more subtle.

This is only to be expected because we know that the early church had a strong tendency to turn to Old Testament prophecies and narratives to understand and interpret the things that Jesus said and did. What we call the Old Testament today was the only Bible that they had. It was the place to which they naturally turned to find answers to anything that puzzled them in the traditions that came down to them. Interpretations of Old Testament passages that illustrated the life of Jesus must have been widely shared and discussed in the early church. They were used at the basis of teaching, instruction and preaching. This means that it is significant that these two gospel writers turn to quite different parts of their Bible to understand Jesus's birth and they never turn to the same passages. This would seem to indicate that, when they came to write, there were no fixed traditions regarding which Old Testament passages applied to the birth of the Messiah.

I won't give an exhaustive list of all the Biblical images that are used in the two gospels, but here are a few key examples:

Old Testament Imagery in Matthew:
- Herod's slaughter of the innocents in Bethlehem has many parallels to the story of the birth of Moses and Pharaoh's attempts to kill him. (Exodus 2:1-10)
- The Magi and the gifts that they bring are connected to the prophecies of Isaiah 60:1-6: "A multitude of camels shall cover you, the young camels of Midian and Ephah; all those from Sheba shall come. They shall bring gold and frankincense, and shall proclaim the praise of the LORD."
- The appearance of the guiding star is likely connected to the "star prophecy" in Numbers 24:17: "A star shall come out of Jacob, and a scepter shall rise out of Israel."
- The virgin birth is explained by and connected to the promise of the coming of Emmanuel by a reference to Isaiah 7:14.
- Joseph's dreams and his interpretations of them are very reminiscent of the story of another Joseph, the son of Jacob, and his dreams in the Old Testament. (Genesis 37

ff.) The parallels between the two Josephs even extend to them both having the same father, Jacob.[67]

Old Testament Imagery in Luke:

- Joseph's return to his ancestral home is connected, I will argue, to the command to celebrate the jubilee in Leviticus 25.
- The key role for the shepherds puts us in mind of prophecies such as the one found in Jeremiah 23:1-8
- The virgin birth (and the birth of John the Baptist) is related to the stories of a number of women in the Old Testament who had difficulty having children—especially Sarah and Hannah. Mary's song of praise in Luke is remarkably close to Hannah's song in 1 Samuel 2:1-10.
- The story of the visit of the Angel Gabriel to Mary and his announcement that she will have a son contains many parallels to the account of the visit of three angels to Abraham and Sarah in Genesis 18.

DEALING WITH THE DIFFERENCES

When you look at the nativity stories in this way, you begin to realize that they disagree with one another far more frequently than they agree, although, it must be acknowledged that many of these differences are not direct contradictions. Saying that the announcement of the birth of Jesus was made to Mary, for example, does not mean that an announcement could not have also been made to Joseph. Whether they are contradictions or not, there is no denying that the two evangelists tell quite different stories— different in tone, in emphasis and in content.

What we have tended to do throughout Christian history is to try to paper over these differences. It is possible, if you really push, to overcome some of these differences and force the birth stories to harmonize with each other. For example, some will argue that you can account for the couple living in a house when the magi arrive in Matthew's gospel by saying that a lot of time has passed (perhaps up to two years) since the birth in the manger that Luke's gospel speaks of, and that the couple has managed to arrange for some permanent housing in the interim. Of course, such a harmonization fails to

---

[67] Matthew 1:16

explain why the couple remained in Bethlehem after the child was born if they only went there briefly to be registered during the census.

Nevertheless, it would seem that, if you push and twist the accounts in certain ways, you can make them harmonize to a certain extent. Perhaps that is fine for some. My problem with such harmonization attempts is this: even if you could make all of these differences go away by pushing and twisting what the individual gospel writers say, you would definitely lose something in the process. You would have distorted your original texts and made them say things that the writers never intended. To accomplish such a feat, you would need to decide that the harmonized account you are aiming for is more important than what each individual evangelist is trying to say. You would lose their distinctive voices.

We are incredibly blessed to have these two nativity stories. They have been left for us by the early church as resources for us to use to learn what it means that Jesus of Nazareth came to live among us and to show us the true nature of the love of God. For that reason we cannot afford to diminish their power. We must be willing to read these texts just as they are and not impose some artificial harmony on them.

For this reason, in order to truly appreciate what Luke is trying to teach us, I choose to read his text as if it were the only account. For the rest of this exploration, while reading what Luke wrote, I will do my best to forget that I ever heard of the visiting magi, the star or King Herod's evil ways. Let's let Luke speak for himself and tell the story on his own terms.

The pretty young girl walks between her parents as they make their way across the village one late summer's day. They are going to a small house with a workshop in its courtyard near the central square where the village synagogue is held. The house is well known because it is the place where the villagers usually go to get their farm tools and implements repaired. The girl, whose name is Mary, is wearing the better of her two dresses and walks with a purposeful stride. She knows that she is going to keep the most important appointment of her young life.

She is nervous, as any girl would be if she were going to meet with the family of her future husband. She is also happy and she has a strong feeling that this is the right thing for her to be doing.

Neither of the two families has a lot. Mary's family has been settled in Nazareth for far longer than anyone can remember. They have their own little plot of land here—land that has been handed down from one generation to the next as a precious trust. In a good year it can produce enough grain, olive oil, figs and wine to keep the family going. In the bad years everyone goes hungry.

There have not been many good years recently.

It doesn't amount to much, but it is the land that God has given to them. When they eat of its produce they give thanks to the God who has been faithful to them for so long.

At least they have land; so many don't any more. Most of the people who have lost their land because of debts and other financial problems fall into the worst of situations. Many are just sold as slaves to cover their debts and lose all freedom and control over their lives.

Others become day labourers which is hardly better. They drift from place to place getting work for a day or two wherever they can find it. Often, ironically, they end up working on the very fields that they had once owned—fields that have been bought by wealthy investors from growing cities like Sepphoris.

There are some families that do marginally better than the landless. They have the talents and skills and, even more important, the valuable tools that allow them to set up shop as artisans. That is what Joseph's family (the family of her intended husband) has done. When they lost their family property in Judea many years previously, they just managed to scrape together the resources to resettle in Nazareth, rent a small house and find work as carpenters.

This certainly does not make them prosperous. They do provide vital services to farmers in the area in exchange for food and they are even able to get occasional work in the city of Sepphoris that Antipas is rebuilding. When things get tight they go just as hungry as anyone else.

An alliance between Mary's family and Joseph's is not particularly advantageous to either party. But in a village like Nazareth, with only a few hundred residents, it is not as if there are that many other prospects. It has been concluded some time ago that the two should marry.

The young people haven't been consulted in this decision. It is a matter to be decided between the two families and their individual desires have little to do with it. Mary and Joseph have known one another for their whole lives. They played together when they were children. As they have grown older, the social restrictions that keep the genders separated have prevented them from speaking together, but they have continued to notice one another and each only sees good things in the other.

Mary is quiet and introspective as she walks towards Joseph's home. This is nothing extraordinary for her. She has very deep thoughts and rarely shares them. She has long watched Joseph and admired him.

He is a young man with strong convictions, a hard worker and one who always insists on doing his very best on any project he is given. All the local people trust in his abilities and often specifically request that he work on a given job. Mary is content with how things have worked out.

The trio arrives at the door and is greeted warmly by Joseph's parents. They enter and share a meal together. After some final details are worked out between the two fathers, the two young people stand before their happy parents, make their promises and pledges and call upon God and their families as their witnesses and helpers.

After all of the promises have been made, Heli, Joseph's father, rises to offer his blessing. He says the kind of thing that people always say on such occasions. He remarks on the beauty of the bride and foretells the birth of many children. When he remarks, as people often do, that great things will come of this union, Mary and Joseph's eyes meet. Though they have not spoken with each other at all before this day and here only formally, there is an instant spark of understanding between the two of them. They both know that Heli's words are truer than he suspects.

Mary leaves the home once again in the company of her parents. She is content to go with them for now but is looking forward to the day when she will not have to return home at all. She looks forward to sharing her life completely with Joseph.

Before that can happen, both of them will have to deal with a few surprises.

Every afternoon after a hard day's work in the fields, Mary's father is in the habit of stopping for a while in the village square for a little cup of wine and a chance to catch up with his friends. Mostly they talk about the weather and how the olive trees are doing and other little matters of everyday life. Occasionally the events going on in the wider world intrude into their discussions: what King Herod Antipas is building up in the huge city of Sepphoris a whole day's walk away, new Roman taxes that are being proposed down south in Judea. Only rarely do they talk about what is happening in the village because nothing ever happens in Nazareth.

The place is far off the beaten track, up in the hills, and nobody ever comes here. In fact, the last interesting thing that happened here was over a generation ago when a new family arrived and settled in. They were refugees from Judea far to the south. They came (according to the rumours that flew everywhere) from the town of Bethlehem. But as refugees from the economic policies of Herod the Great, they had brought almost nothing with them— only a few basic tools that allowed them to scrape out a living as carpenters in the local region.

As is always the case in a small village where nothing ever changes, it wasn't easy for the new family to fit in. People who have known them for decades now, whose children have grown up with theirs, still treat them like outsiders. But they are good people and the village has gradually warmed to them. In fact the next big event that is expected to happen in the village is a marriage. Joseph, the young son of the "new" family is to marry Mary. Her father is very pleased with the match that he has made for his daughter for, though his family is even poorer than most in Nazareth,

Joseph is a fine young man and he has every confidence that he will do well by Mary.

One day when Mary's father stops by the square, his friends have plenty to talk about for a stranger has appeared that very day in the village. Everyone is busy speculating about him and gossiping about him. They say he must have come from the south because he speaks with a strange accent. He is dressed far too shabbily to be a merchant or a traveling nobleman and so it has been concluded that he must be a homeless wanderer or perhaps even an escaped slave. He is not, in other words, the kind of person that anyone wants around. Why he might even be a rebel or a bandit and welcoming someone like that can be very dangerous these days.

That is why everyone has been going out of their way to make the young (and, admittedly, very handsome) man feel most unwelcome in Nazareth. They are just hoping that he will get the message and move on as quickly as possible.

As soon as he hears the tale, Mary's father, knows that this is just not the right reaction. He immediately sets out to find the man. It does not take long, Nazareth, after all, is not a big place.

When he finds him he immediately bows down low to the ground and says, "Please, sir, you would do my family a great honour if only you would consent to come and lay down your belongings in our house this night and allow us to share our bread for this day." So gracious is the invitation that the stranger must accept.

When her father arrives with the stranger, Mary is the only one at home. She is just returning from the well with water to prepare the evening meal. Her mother is still at work in the fields with the other women, her brothers are likewise occupied. Once he has installed the stranger in the kitchen, Mary's father hurries out to meet her at the door.

"Daughter," he says, "there was a man in the village. He had no place to go and no one would welcome him and so I have brought him here to share our table tonight."

Mary nods but she cannot keep surprise and even a bit of fear from showing on her face. She has always been a quiet and dutiful child but she cannot believe that her father has invited a complete stranger into their home.

"Father," she has to say, "you know what mother will think about you inviting such a man as this into our home. We are living in dangerous times—times when associations with the wrong kinds of people can mean a death sentence. She would call this foolishness and she would be right."

"Mary, Mary, Mary, your mother is a very wise woman, I know, but she would be wrong about this. Everyone in Nazareth is wrong. Come on, you know the story. I've told is to you often enough. It was your favourite when you were seven."

"What story?" Mary asks.

"About the time when Father Abraham was sitting outside his tent..."

"Ah yes," Mary interrupts, "and three men came along."

"Three strangers," adds her father, "complete strangers that he knew nothing about. And yet Abraham did not hesitate to greet them as lords and treat them with honour. He invited them to sit under a tree and asked his wife to prepare them a meal."

"Yes, I remember," says Mary, "and Sarah made three barley cakes and served them with a fine calf and curds and whey—a feast fit for a king!"

"That is right, Mary. But then, as they ate together, something amazing happened, didn't it?"

"Oh yes," Mary's eyes flash, "Abraham and Sarah discovered that these men weren't strangers at all. In fact, in the midst of the meal they discovered that it was God who had been there all along. And that's not all. The Lord even made a promise to Sarah that she would have a son. Sarah laughed at the very idea. It was impossible because she was so old! But God's promise was fulfilled."

"Yes, dear child, it was. God's promises are always sure. And that was how they knew for sure that God had visited them. And because Abraham and Sarah encountered God by welcoming strangers, in my household we will never turn one away. You never know who you might be turning away."

"But surely, Father, you don't think that this man is some kind of heavenly visitor do you?"

Her father's chuckle is a low rumble in the back of his throat. "No, my daughter. I'm sure he's just another man who has lost everything and is reduced to wandering. But while this house remains mine, we will welcome him as if he were Herod Antipas himself. Now, you go and take him a cup of wine and a barley cake while I see what kind of meal we can put together out back."

As she enters the kitchen with the cup of wine, Mary resolves that she will not speak to the stranger, that she will not even lift her eyes to look upon him. It is her duty to serve him as her father has commanded, but she will do it with all modesty and humility as is fitting for a young woman of Nazareth.

Of course, it never occurs to her that he might notice her, much less speak to her. Men are trained all their lives to believe that a woman is of no account and has nothing important to say. That is why she jumps (almost spilling the wine) when he turns and looks straight at her with a piercing glance.

"Greetings," he says, "you are indeed highly favoured! The Lord is with you."

Mary doesn't know what to make of such a greeting. For a moment she thinks he is mocking her, but he looks at her so seriously that she dares not laugh. She doesn't know what to say and so she lets him continue.

"Do not be afraid, Mary, for you have found favour with God. You will conceive and bear a son." He even goes on from there to tell her what name she ought to give to such a son.

Now that is ridiculous! She knows very well that she is not about to have a son no matter what he is called! And, speaking of names, how does he know hers? She is sure her father hasn't mentioned it to him.

Mary can't help but laugh now. "A child?" she says, "Me? That's impossible! I am a virgin!"

"You laugh," says the stranger. "I remember another who laughed as well."

An odd thrill passes through Mary's whole body. She was suddenly fully awake and aware of everything around her. She just knows that she is in the presence of something that she cannot quite explain.

The stranger continues: "Mary, you need to learn what she learned: that nothing is impossible when God is involved."

Mary has no response to that and so she retreats into the humility that had been drilled into her since birth. "Sir," she says, "I am nothing but a simple servant."

But at that moment she feels a strange surge of boldness pass through her and she lifts her eyes to meet his. "But I will serve the Lord and be a slave to no one else."

At this the stranger merely nods and seems quite satisfied. Mary flees the room in confusion while he sips his wine.

When she returns to the room but a few minutes later, the man is gone. She does not see him again—no one does. They enquire throughout the village the next day but it seems that he has stayed in no other home. There is no trace of him at all. He has simply disappeared.

Mary ponders long and hard at the meaning of her strange conversation with the man. But that day she only has one question for her father.

"Did he say where he was from, Father? What was his family and his name?" she wants to know.

"Of his village and family he would tell me nothing, my daughter. But as for his name, he called himself Gabriel."

3) WHEN IS LUKE SAYING THAT JESUS WAS BORN?

Now that we have agreed to set aside, for the moment, Matthew's birth narrative and try to understand Luke's account on its own terms, we may turn to the question of Luke's dating of the events. *When* is Luke saying that Jesus was born? Answering this question is important, but not because it will allow us to establish the actual birth date of Jesus. After all, if Matthew and Luke disagree on the date, we may have no way of establishing which one is correct. Indeed, their failure to agree may be an indication that neither one has enough information to be certain of Jesus's birth date.

We do not know what time of year it was when Jesus was born. Neither of the two evangelists gives any indication that he knows the month or season in which the birth took place. The closest Luke comes is to tell us that when Jesus was born "there were shepherds living in the fields, keeping watch over their flock by night."[68] This seems to suggest that it was spring or possibly summer because, in the cooler months, shepherds would be inclined to keep the sheep closer to the fold, but it is hardly a clear indication. Clearly the date on the annual calendar is not an important matter for the gospel writers which probably indicates that there was no interest in the church of their day in celebrating a festival in honour of the birth of Christ. The December 25 date for the birth of Jesus came to be established by the church much later for a number of reasons but those reasons had nothing to do with what is written in the birth accounts.

What we want to establish, at least roughly, is what year it was as far as Luke is concerned. This is an important thing to do because Luke seems to use his historical setting to communicate his understanding of the meaning of Jesus's birth. Certainly he takes great care to date Jesus's birth and the beginning of his ministry relative to the things that were going on in the world at those times. He makes precise references to such things as the census, the governorship of Quirinius and, later, the rule of Tiberius Caesar and the governorship of Pontius Pilate. The fact that he takes such care over these details is an indication that he found meaning and

---

[68] Luke 2:8

significance in those times and events. To discover that meaning for ourselves, therefore, we will need to have an understanding of the events that Luke sees taking place in the world as Jesus is born.

The question is this: has the existence of Matthew's nativity story with its very important and memorable role for Herod the Great made us misread Luke's story and assume that he is also saying that Jesus must have been born sometime between 8 and 4 BCE? If we take Matthew's account away, and read Luke's gospel on its own merits, will we come to the conclusion that he is saying that Jesus was born during a different period of time?

We have already discussed the dating of the census to which Luke refers. It certainly seems as if the best candidate for the census that Luke describes—a "first" census that was taken during the governorship of Quirinius and one that was about including Judea in "all the world" (that is, the Roman world)—is the census that was taken in 6 CE. This alone suggests that Luke is working under the assumption that Jesus was born around that time. But, it is certainly not conclusive. After all, it could still be possible that Luke is aware of another census—one that escaped all historical notice but that was somehow still well-known at the time that this gospel was written—that fits the description that he gives in his gospel. We must ask if there are any other indications of a date of birth for Jesus in Luke's writings.

THERE WAS A PRIEST NAMED ZECHARIAH

In fact, Luke begins his gospel with a reference to an historical era. Immediately after his prologue, he begins his account by saying,

> In the days of King Herod of Judea, there was a
> priest named Zechariah, who belonged to the
> priestly order of Abijah. His wife was a descendant
> of Aaron, and her name was Elizabeth. Both of
> them were righteous before God, living blamelessly
> according to all the commandments and
> regulations of the Lord. But they had no children,
> because Elizabeth was barren, and both were
> getting on in years.[69]

Although there are, of course, a number of King Herods in Jewish history, this appears to be a clear reference to the reign of

---

[69] Luke 1:5-7

Herod the Great who died in the spring of 4 BCE. Since Zechariah and Elizabeth are the parents of John the Baptist and since we learn as the chapter progresses that both Elizabeth and Mary the mother of Jesus were pregnant at the same time, this has led to the conclusion that the Gospel of Luke agrees with the Gospel of Matthew that Jesus was born during the reign of Herod.

I would argue that this dating is hardly conclusive. All that Luke tells us is that Zechariah was a minor priest while Herod was king. He then goes on to recount the long term infertility and advancing age of both Zechariah and his wife. The Biblical parallel he has in mind is clearly the story of Abraham and Sarah and, according to the book of Genesis, Sarah was barren for 25 years before having her child. It was from the time that Abraham was 75 to the time that he was 100.[70] Now, of course, Luke cannot have such a long period of time in mind for Zechariah and Elizabeth, but the infertility he is talking about must have lasted for a significant period of time.

He is presenting us, not just with a brief moment in the life of this couple, but with an extended episode. Though his intention may be to say that Zechariah *became* a priest during the reign of Herod and *served* in the temple during Herod's life, that hardly needs to mean that everything that happened to him, including the birth of his son, happened under Herod. Zechariah could well have become a priest in about 5 BCE and attempted to have a child with Elizabeth for a decade before eventually having a son.

During the reign of Herod the Great, the king exercised the right to nominate the Chief Priest of the temple in Jerusalem. Herod's choices were often very controversial. Henk Jagersma says this about Herod's dealings with the priests:

> Herod also nominated and deposed high priests at will. For high priests he chose people who were well disposed towards him and took little notice of existing traditions. This way of carrying on did not do much for the respect of this old institution. It can also be assumed that Herod's action widened the gulf between the people and the priests. Even apart from this, the reputation of the priests continued to sink in an uninterrupted decline.[71]

---

[70] Genesis 12:4; 21:5
[71] Jagersma, p. 111.

Herod would not have been involved in naming such a minor priest as Zechariah seems to be. Nevertheless, Luke could be adhering to a tradition here—the tradition of associating a priest's service with the king who reigned when he was ordained into the office.

It is also significant that Luke highlights the righteousness and blamelessness of Zechariah. If the priests who served during the time of Herod were universally believed to be corrupt, this establishes Zechariah in contrast to the chief priests who were named by Herod. This may be the point of mentioning Herod's era at the beginning of the story of Zechariah and Elizabeth but it may not have all that much to do with the events immediately surrounding the birth of John.

A POORLY INTEGRATED STORY

There is one other thing we should notice about the story of Zechariah and Elizabeth. It is very hard to know how to relate that story, recounted in the first and longest chapter of Gospel of Luke, to the rest of his book. There are a number of ideas and themes that are introduced in the first chapter that the writer does not develop in the rest of the gospel.

Most importantly, Luke tells us in the first chapter that there was a blood relationship between Jesus of Nazareth and John the Baptist as Jesus's mother was a relative of the mother of John.[72] This is an interesting and potentially very meaningful revelation. But, strangely, Luke never elaborates on it. In the rest of the gospel, in fact, he never mentions this relationship again. In the first chapter Luke describes a foetal meeting between these two spiritual giants of the first century—tells us that John the Baptist "leapt in [Elizabeth's] womb" on hearing Mary's voice.[73] He seems to be promising to talk about a lifelong association between these two preachers.

If that is the case, Luke certainly does not follow through on that promise. Luke, alone among all the gospels, does not describe any meeting at all between these two men apart from that meeting in the womb. He does *imply* that Jesus was baptised by John, but he strangely avoids saying so directly.[74] This leaves the impression,

---

[72] Luke 1:36
[73] Luke 1:41
[74] Luke 3:21. See below for discussion of this verse.

58

throughout the rest of this gospel, that Jesus and John really only knew one another by reputation.

There is an even more tantalizing idea that is put forward in the first chapter on which Luke does not elaborate. Elizabeth, the mother of John, is particularly singled out as a descendant of Aaron, the brother of Moses and the first high priest.[75] When Mary, Jesus's mother, is identified as Elizabeth's relative, it is reasonable to assume that she too must be descended from that same distinguished ancestor.

Luke, like the other evangelists, makes much of the fact that Jesus was a "son of David." In the first century it was considered to be essential by many that the Messiah be a descendant of King David and Luke dutifully records this fact and even provides a genealogy to support the claim. Luke also specifies that Jesus received this descent through his father Joseph (even though he is careful to say that Jesus was only assumed to be the son of Joseph).[76] In the first chapter he also drops this hint that Jesus might also have been descended on his mother's side from Aaron the High Priest. And there was surely no doubt as to who was truly his mother!

Now it would be hard to imagine more convincing credentials for a Jewish messiah than that he be descended on one side from King David and on the other from Aaron, the first high priest. That would put Jesus in a totally different league from all the other first century claimants to that exalted title. Why doesn't Luke follow up on this suggestion anywhere else in the gospel? Not even as he recounts Jesus dealings with the chief priests in Jerusalem before his death does Luke renew the suggestion that Jesus is himself descended from a line of priests.

Why does Luke not follow through on these interesting ideas that are presented in the first chapter of his gospel? It is as if everything that is mentioned in Chapter 1 is forgotten in the rest of the book.

I might suggest that the first chapter was added to the book by someone else, but such an explanation would not stand scrutiny. There is no reason to think that this first chapter came from another hand. In terms of style, themes and vocabulary it is not very different from the rest of the gospel. For example, the story of the extraordinary events around the birth of John the Baptist ends with this description of the reaction:

---

[75] Luke 1:5
[76] Luke 3:23

Fear came over all their neighbours, and all these
things were talked about throughout the entire hill
country of Judea. All who heard them pondered
them and said, "What then will this child become?"
For, indeed, the hand of the Lord was with him.[77]

This is the kind of reaction that Luke often reports in very
similar ways after extraordinary events in the rest of the gospel.[78]

In terms of style, chapter 1 seems to be Lukan, but the content
is not very well integrated with the rest of the gospel. It seems to me
that, for whatever reason, Luke felt little need to relate his story of
the birth of John the Baptist with the rest of his account. Perhaps
the basic material for this chapter came to him late in the writing
process—perhaps they were even drawn from traditions that had
developed among the followers of John the Baptist (for Luke does
indeed claim to know something about a follower of John the
Baptist named Apollos many years after John's death).[79] It would
seem that Luke just took the material, rewrote it in his own style and
never bothered to relate the story with anything else that he wrote
about Jesus.

All this is to suggest that, even if Luke did mean to say that
John was born during the reign of Herod the Great, he might not
have cared all that much if that fact clashed with or even
contradicted the date for the birth of Jesus that he offered in his
second chapter and in the rest of his gospel.

At the very least, it would seem that the brief mention of the
reign of King Herod in Luke 1:5 isn't really enough to convince us
that Luke clearly intended to say that Jesus was born during the time
of Herod the Great. I am convinced that, if it were not for the
Matthew's nativity story and the emphasis that it puts on Herod's
reign, interpreters would never have given so much weight to Luke's
passing reference to the reign of Herod the Great at the beginning
of his gospel.

In the Fifteenth Year of Tiberius

Luke also provides us with a date for the beginning of the
ministry of John the Baptist. It is a date that is much more precise
than any other date in this gospel:

---

[77] Luke 1:65-66
[78] E.g. Luke 2:20; 4:36-37; 7:16,17; 18:43
[79] Acts 18:24, 25

> In the fifteenth year of the reign of Emperor
> Tiberius, when Pontius Pilate was governor of
> Judea, and Herod [that is, Herod Antipas] was ruler
> of Galilee, and his brother Philip ruler of the
> region of Ituraea and Trachonitis, and Lysanias
> ruler of Abilene, during the high priesthood of
> Annas and Caiaphas, the word of God came to
> John son of Zechariah in the wilderness.[80]

Of course the dates of the rule of Emperor Tiberius are very well documented and we know that he ascended the imperial throne upon the death of Caesar Augustus in 14 CE. Therefore, Luke is stating quite unambiguously that the ministry of John the Baptist began around 29 CE. Note that he is clearly speaking of the beginning of John's preaching—the moment when the word of God came to him. It would have taken time for him to gain a following especially as he started out in the wilderness and far from large centres such as Jerusalem. It certainly would have taken quite a while for him to baptise "all the people" as Luke puts it.[81] So how long does Luke understand that John carried out his ministry before Jesus came along?

Certainly Luke is quite aware that John the Baptist had a ministry that had a big impact independent of anything that Jesus did. In the Book of Acts he makes reference to the fact that it was quite possible to preach the "way of the Lord" without knowing anything about Jesus—by only making reference to John the Baptist.[82] So it is only reasonable to assume that Luke would place the beginning of the ministry of John the Baptist somewhat before the beginning of the ministry of Jesus. Yes, they were contemporaries, but John was considered, for a while at least, to be the senior prophet.

This is confirmed by John's baptism of Jesus. Actually, Luke appears to be somewhat uncomfortable with the fact that John baptized Jesus. While the gospels of Matthew and Mark simply acknowledge that this is what happened, Luke actually hesitates to admit it. He can only say, "Now when all the people were baptized, and when Jesus also had been baptized..."[83] He seems to go out of his way to avoid actually saying that Jesus's baptism was performed

---

[80] Luke 3:1,2 with notes.
[81] v. 21
[82] Acts 18:24,25
[83] Luke 3:21

by John. It is not surprising that Luke should give only a grudging admission of Jesus's baptism by John because it implies that John was more important than Jesus. Luke believed that no one was more important than Jesus. That is why he plays down the importance of the baptism.

Luke may also be doing the same thing when he talks about the ministry of John preceding the ministry of Jesus. He knows very well that John was preaching and had a large following for a while before Jesus came on the scene, but he doesn't want to dwell on this point because it gives John seniority over Jesus. Perhaps that is why so many people who have read Luke 3:1-23 have come away with the impression that the ministries of John and Jesus began at approximately the same time.

But there must have been a gap. Of course, it would be very helpful if we could establish by exactly how much time the ministry of John preceded the ministry of Jesus because Luke writes, "Jesus was about thirty years old when he began his work."[84] If we could establish when Luke is saying that Jesus began his ministry, it would therefore also give us a rough idea of when Luke is saying that Jesus was born. Unfortunately, we are given no specific information about the period of time between the two preachers.

If we were to presume that Jesus began his work about four years after the word of God first came to John, that would mean that he began preaching around 33 CE. If Jesus was born during the census of 6 CE, how old would he be in 33 CE? He would be 27 years old. In my opinion, that would qualify as "about thirty." If, on the other hand, Luke is thinking that Jesus was born in 6 BCE, the commonly accepted date based on Matthew's nativity story, by 33 CE Jesus would be 38 years old and that sounds more like *about 40* to me! Therefore I would argue that Luke's clear dating of the beginning of the preaching of John the Baptist to the fifteenth year of the reign of Tiberius only confirms that he is thinking of a birth date for Jesus sometime around 6 CE.

JUDAS THE GALILEAN ROSE UP

There is a third Lucan text that may be helpful in understanding his sense of the chronology of Jesus's life. In the fifth chapter of Acts, Luke gives a report on a discussion held in the Sanhedrin— the assembly of Jewish elders in Jerusalem. The council has arrested

---

[84] Luke 3:23

Peter and some of the other apostles and is trying to decide what to do with them. They send the disciples out of the room in order that they may discuss their fate in private.

Obviously, if the Sanhedrin is meeting in private, Luke really has no way of knowing exactly what was really said in that meeting. But historical writers in the ancient world never hesitated to provide the full texts of speeches and conversations even when they did not have reliable sources. And Luke believed that he had an extra source of information: the inspiration of the Holy Spirit. He would have had no trouble saying that the Spirit told him what was said behind those closed doors. But that does not mean that the Spirit would necessarily reveal what was *actually* said in the secret meeting.

Evangelists like Luke believed that they were inspired when they wrote their accounts, but inspiration is hardly a precise process. I think it is important not to have a view of it that is too narrow. How can we really explain such a phenomenon? Even neurologists and psychologists struggle to explain the mechanism that causes a person to be inspired—to come up with a thought that no one has thought before or to see something from a truly unique point of view.

Let me suggest one way to look at it. Inspiration is a gift that most people experience to varying degrees. It allows us to see things from very creative angles, to understand, not merely what was said or done in a particular situation, but to see the meaning behind such things. I know that others might understand such a process from a purely neurological point of view as chemical reactions taking place in the brain, but I tend to understand that *all* forms of inspiration are ultimately divine in origin (even if they manifest themselves in the form of chemical reactions that take place in the brain).

Luke is speaking to us through the mechanism of inspired imagination. That is why, in the speeches that follow, we need to understand that what Luke is offering us is not exactly what the elders of the Sanhedrin said. Luke's inspired imagination gives him access to much more important information than that. Luke is reporting to us what the Spirit has told him that they *must have* said or, perhaps, what they *could have* said and, most importantly, what their deliberations *meant*:

> When they heard this, they were enraged and
> wanted to kill them. But a Pharisee in the council
> named Gamaliel, a teacher of the law, respected by
> all the people, stood up and ordered the men to be
> put outside for a short time. Then he said to them,

"Fellow Israelites, consider carefully what you propose to do to these men. For some time ago Theudas rose up, claiming to be somebody, and a number of men, about four hundred, joined him; but he was killed, and all who followed him were dispersed and disappeared. After him Judas the Galilean rose up at the time of the census and got people to follow him; he also perished, and all who followed him were scattered. So in the present case, I tell you, keep away from these men and let them alone; because if this plan or this undertaking is of human origin, it will fail; but if it is of God, you will not be able to overthrow them—in that case you may even be found fighting against God!"[85]

The first thing we note is this: Luke, using the voice of Gamaliel, makes reference to what he calls "*the* census." He doesn't say "*a* census" or "*one of the* censuses." He uses the definite article. Either Luke is only aware of one historical census or, more likely, he thinks that there is only one census that really matters. He surely must be thinking of the very same census that he mentions near the beginning of his gospel. In Luke chapter two he tells us only that the census he is interested in was taken following a decree of Augustus, during the governorship of Quirinius and that it was the first or initial census. But here we are given an additional piece of information: there was a rebellion led by Judas the Galilean during this census.

I have already cited the section in Josephus's *Antiquities of the Jews* where he describes the census that was taken in 6 CE. After what I have already quoted, Josephus goes on to speak of this same Judas and his rebellion.[86] It would appear that in this passage from the Book of Acts we have another confirmation that, as far as Luke is concerned, Jesus was born during the census of 6 CE.

Luke's mention of Judas also raises some other issues that we will have to examine. Surely, it is not insignificant that Luke is aware that (at the very moment when he says Mary and Joseph left Nazareth, in Galilee, to go to Bethlehem) Galilee just happened to be at the centre of a major revolt against Rome while the Judean census was being conducted. It is one thing for a couple to make a

---

[85] Acts 5:33-39. Emphasis added.
[86] Josephus, *Antiquities of the Jews*, 18:2-4. We will look in greater depth into Judas's career later.

long and potentially dangerous journey during a time of peace, but it is quite another thing for them to do so in the midst of an uprising!

For the moment, it is enough to recognize that, in this passage, Luke is continuing to think of the date of birth as occurring sometime around 6 CE—the year of *the* census, the year when Quirinius governed and the year when Judas rebelled.

WHEN IS LUKE ASSUMING THAT JESUS WAS BORN?

All of these considerations lead me to the conclusion that, if we had never had the Gospel of Matthew to lead people to think that Jesus had been born before the death of Herod the Great in 4 BCE and if all we had ever had to go by was the Gospel of Luke, no one would have ever argued that Jesus was born so early.

None of this can really help us to establish exactly when Jesus was born. All we can really say at this point is that Matthew and Luke are working according to different assumptions regarding his date of birth. I suspect, in fact, that neither of these two authors really has much solid information to establish a birth date for Christ. Any such details would have likely been quite sketchy by the time these gospels were written. If these writers did not have good information on the details of the birth of Jesus in their source material, they would have had another place to look to find what they considered to be perfectly reliable information. These writers, as faithful Christians, believed that the Old Testament had foretold just about every aspect of Jesus's life and ministry. When they had any holes in their narrative that they needed to fill, they would not have hesitated to draw upon Old Testament passages to supply them with the information they needed.

Matthew's birth narrative is an excellent example of this process. Many have remarked that, throughout his Gospel, Matthew takes great pains to present Jesus as a new Moses. For example, Matthew tells us that Jesus gave his most important sermon, a new Law, from the top of a mountain[87] just as Moses gave the first Law to Israel from the top of Mount Sinai.[88] Matthew also records five major discourses of Jesus spread throughout the gospel. This corresponds to the five books in the Old Testament traditionally known as the five books of Moses: Genesis, Exodus, Leviticus,

---

[87] Matthew 5-7
[88] Exodus 19 ff

Numbers and Deuteronomy. These are but two of the most obvious ways in which Matthew presents Jesus as a new Moses.

Matthew considered that one of his tasks as an evangelist was to show the link between Jesus and Moses. Therefore it is only natural that he should assume, given no particular information to the contrary, that Jesus must have been born in a way reminiscent of the birth of Moses which is related in Exodus 2:1-10. Because of what he believed about the prophetic nature of Scripture, Matthew *knew* that Jesus must have had a birth like Moses's birth—that is to say a birth overshadowed by a vicious tyrant who was determined to destroy the threat that was contained in the newborn child, and so Matthew looked through the recent history of Judea to find a tyrant like the Pharaoh who had tried to put the baby Moses to death. He would not have taken very long to find Herod the Great, a monarch renowned for his ruthlessness and bloodthirstiness. For Matthew, the conclusion was simple: Jesus must have been born during the rule of Herod, and so Matthew sets about filling in the gaps in his story by drawing on the book of Exodus and on other sources about Moses in Jewish tradition.

One of the other sources that Matthew used may well be reflected in the following passage from Josephus's *Antiquities of the Jews* regarding the birth of Moses. Here we see a tradition that was known at the time Matthew was writing his Gospel indicating that Pharaoh's slaughter of the Hebrew children was prompted by him hearing a prophecy of the birth of a saviour. It certainly sounds very much like Herod in the second chapter of the Gospel of Matthew:

> While the affairs of the Hebrews were in this
> condition, there was this occasion offered itself to
> the Egyptians, which made them more solicitous
> for the extinction of our nation. One of those
> sacred scribes, who are very sagacious in foretelling
> future events, truly told the king, that about this
> time there would be born a child to the Israelites,
> who, if he were reared, would bring the Egyptian
> dominion low, and would raise the Israelites; that
> he would excel all men in virtue, and obtain a glory
> that would be remembered through all ages. Which
> thing was so feared by the king, that, according to
> this man's opinion, he commanded that they
> should cast every male child, who was born to the
> Israelites, into the river, and kill it; that besides this,
> the Egyptian midwives should watch the labours of

66

the Hebrew women, and observe what is born, for those were the women who were enjoined to do the office of midwives to them; and by reason of their relation to the king, would not transgress his commands. He enjoined also, that if any parents should disobey him, and venture to save their male children alive, they and their families should be killed.[89]

It is not too hard to see how Matthew could have taken the story of Moses as told in Exodus and in other Jewish traditions and applied it directly to his story of the birth of Jesus. Now we can understand what might have led him to set the story of Jesus's birth during the reign of Herod.

All of this suggests that, if we really want to understand the birth story that Luke is telling in his Gospel, we need to understand what Old Testament passages he has in mind as he writes. Is there any possibility that, by examining the Old Testament passages that Luke turns to fill the gaps of his birth story, we can see why Luke sets his birth narrative during a certain census? To answer that question we turn to a major Old Testament theme that runs through Luke's Gospel (much like the idea of Jesus as a new Moses runs through Matthew's). I refer to the idea of jubilee.

---

[89] Josephus, *Antiquities of the Jews* 2:205-207

There is nothing left but smouldering ruins. The village looks as if it had been about the size of Nazareth and that fact alone makes a shiver run down both Mary and Joseph's back. They walk forward in silence, their mouths gaping at all the senseless destruction that they see.

"Why?" Mary demands. "Who would do something like this? What possible reason could they have to destroy like this?" But Joseph is the only one there and he can offer her no explanation. He finds the whole thing just as bewildering as she does.

They make their way through the centre of the village—what used to be a village—passing by a central plaza. It was a Jewish village; they can tell by the marks on many doorposts of the houses and by other subtle signs that only another Jew would notice. They can't help but imagine how the people here must have met each sabbath in this plaza to hear the scriptures and to pray. Now all they find in the centre of the plaza is a Roman spear planted in the ground—a stark and ominous sign.

At the far end of the village they finally see someone. He is an old man. His clothes are torn and his head is covered with ashes. He walks about almost in a trance but when Joseph calls to him, he approaches.

"What has happened here?" Joseph asks the man gently. "Who has done this evil thing?"

"It was the Romans, who else?" says the man. He almost spits the words out. "They came with their swords and with their fire and they destroyed everything. They have killed all my family. They left only me. It was not out of kindness!

"They said we had ties to Judas of Galilee, the rebel leader. And, who knows, perhaps it was true that some of the families here had been supplying Judas's men. I don't think it mattered much to them whether it was true or not. They were looking to make a statement."

"They certainly have made one," Mary says.

"They told me that I was to tell everyone who passed this way what they had done and why," the man continues. "They say that they will do the same to anyone who supports the rebels or who even listens to their ideas."

Joseph and Mary look at each other, wordlessly agreeing that they will not say a word about their home village or their destination.

They can say or do nothing to console the man in his loss. They invite him to share in their meagre evening meal, but once the meal is over, they pack up quickly and move on, eager to put distance between themselves and this village of death.

4) THE OLD TESTAMENT IDEAL OF JUBILEE

In five long chapters, the Book of Joshua lays out the territories of the various tribes of Israel in mind-numbing detail—clan by clan.[90] It all seems so pointless and dull to us as modern readers. But the allotment of land and how it was shared out among all the people was obviously a very important concern for these people. It was a matter of life or death.

The land was considered to be a gift of God. It was the land that had been promised to them since the times of the patriarchs. Yet God had not simply given it to them. The Book of Joshua tells the story of how they took the land from the people who happened to be already living there through violence and conquest.

The gift of the land was also conditional. Possession of the land was not automatic and the people were required to live according the laws and commands of God in order to maintain their ownership of it.[91] Thus the people were never to forget who the true owner of that land was.

The ancient nation of Israel and its economy was built around the idea that every man had been given his own little piece of land by God. This was a very patriarchal society and women were not permitted to possess or inherit land except under extraordinary circumstances, and even then they were put under severe restrictions. The daughters of Zelophehad, for example, were allowed to inherit their father's property because he had no sons but, to prevent the land from passing out of the possession of Zelophehad's clan, the daughters were required to marry only within the clan.[92]

Such a society was flawed in that it failed to recognize the true value and dignity of women but it did still seek to meet the basic needs of all the men, women and children through this ownership of land. Every man was supposed to be responsible for the care of an entire household. Ownership of the land, therefore, was not for the purpose of sustaining individuals but entire families. The idea was that each family would provide for its own needs through subsistence farming upon the land that was theirs. According to this

[90] Joshua 13ff
[91] Deuteronomy 8
[92] Numbers 27:1-11. See also Numbers 36:1-12

ideal, no family would have access to enough resources to become wealthy, but everyone would have what they needed to sustain themselves.

The land was to remain in the possession of these families of Israel in perpetuity. They could not sell or transfer their land to anyone else.[93] Even if they wanted to, the Law would not permit them to leave their land in the hands of anyone else. This was seen as necessary because the land was God's way of providing for the basic needs of his people. It was the ideal—the way that it was supposed to be. As the Biblical formula put it, "Every man will sit under *his own* vine and under *his own* fig tree, and no one will make them afraid."[94] Land ownership and the ability of families to subsist on that land were to be the norm.

But, as we all know, reality has a way of getting in the way of ideals. When a family is just subsisting (living from hand to mouth) there are so many things that can go wrong. A few bad harvests, a plague of locusts, an army or a band of raiders passing through the territory or any number of other disasters can make the difference between just getting by and starvation. Bad things did happen and sometimes forced people to borrow heavily, using their land as collateral, just to survive. When things got worse, people could be forced to forfeit or sell their land. In extreme cases, they might have no choice but to sell themselves and their families into slavery.

Unforeseeable disasters were not the only threat to this ideal. There seems to be a natural human tendency, at least on the part of some, to become discontented with mere subsistence, and so there were some Israelites who wanted more. They would take advantage of the bad things that happened to their neighbours to accumulate wealth, land and slaves for themselves. They would take control of large tracts of land and put them together into efficient farms, often using the newly available slaves as their workforce.

One of the ways they did this was through debt, which has always been a very popular way to transfer more wealth to those who already have some. They would happily lend to their neighbours when they were in need, charging a high rate of interest. Then, when their neighbours could not repay their debts, they would take their land or their freedom or both. For this reason, the

---

[93] Numbers 36:7; 1 Kings 21:3

[94] Micah 4:4 (*New International Version*), emphasis added. This same image of the vine and fig tree is repeated several times in the Bible. See 1 Kings 4:25, 2 Kings 18:31, Isaiah 36:16 and Zechariah 3:10. John 1:48 may also be a reference to this ideal.

Bible puts very strict controls on debts and the charging of interest on loans.[95] In addition, there is a provision to simply cancel all debts every seven years, during what is called the year of sabbath.[96]

Despite all of these regulations (which may not have always been strictly followed), inequality among Israelites still occurred over time. Families lost the land that had been in their families for generations, land that been given to them, they believed, by God. Over time the people of Israel shared the land less and less in the way that God had intended. Something was required to restore the balance: a year of jubilee.

The Israelites were to count seven "weeks" of years (that is, 49 years) and when the seventh sabbath year had been celebrated they were to sound the *shofar*, a trumpet made out of a ram's horn, throughout the whole land.[97] Riders and messengers must have been sent out to each town and village throughout the land to sound the horns and announce the good news to the poor. Then, once everyone had been informed, the year of jubilee would begin with the next year, the fiftieth. During this year two key things would happen.

THE RETURN

The first and most important command during the year of jubilee was this: "In this year of jubilee you shall return, every one of you, to your property."[98] The word *property* in the Hebrew of this passage refers specifically to the property one might inherit from one's family. It is the same Hebrew word that is used in a key passage dealing with property rights in the Book of Ezekiel where the NRSV translates it as *possession*:

> "The prince shall not take from the people's
> inheritance, thrusting them out of their possession;
> he shall give his sons inheritance from his own
> possession so that My people will not be scattered,
> anyone from his possession."[99]

This command to return to the ancestral property seems to have had two dimensions. First of all, it was a holy festival. All of

---

[95] E.g. Exodus 22:25
[96] Deuteronomy 15
[97] Leviticus 25:9
[98] Leviticus 25:13
[99] Ezekiel 46:18. Emphasis added.

the people were to celebrate God's gift of the land to the families of Israel by dropping whatever they were doing and returning from wherever they might be to the land that was rightfully theirs, the land on which all their ancestors once lived. It was a kind of nation-wide homecoming festival.

But this returning had more meaning to it than just a mere visit back home. By returning there, these families were also laying claim to their heritage. In many cases, this would just be a matter of publically confirming this ownership. Where there had been difficulties and the land had been sold or lost in some other way, the rightful owners had the right to take back what was theirs:

> If anyone of your kin falls into difficulty and sells a
> piece of property, then the next of kin shall come
> and redeem what the relative has sold. If the
> person has no one to redeem it, but then prospers
> and finds sufficient means to do so, the years since
> its sale shall be computed and the difference shall
> be refunded to the person to whom it was sold,
> and the property shall be returned. But if there are
> not sufficient means to recover it, what was sold
> shall remain with the purchaser until the year of
> jubilee; in the jubilee it shall be released, and the
> property shall be returned.[100]

The law of the jubilee attempted to give due consideration to the purchaser of the property and to see that he was reimbursed fairly, but the bottom line was not negotiable: "In the jubilee it shall be released, and the property shall be returned." There were no other options. By the end of the jubilee every Israelite family had to be resettled on the land that God had given it.

THE RELEASE

The second key command of the jubilee year was a necessary addition to the first: all slaves were to be released. For what was the use of each Israelite male reclaiming his land if he did not have his freedom to live on it?[101] The law goes through the various ways that an Israelite might be released from service to another Israelite or to

---

[100] Leviticus 25:25-28

[101] Since land ownership in Ancient Israel was an exclusive male right, I use the male pronoun.

a resident alien. But, again, the bottom line was that freedom must be given in that year:

> And if they have not been redeemed in any of
> these ways, they and their children with them shall
> go free in the jubilee year. For to me the people of
> Israel are servants; they are my servants whom I
> brought out from the land of Egypt: I am the
> LORD your God.[102]

Just as the right to return to one's ancestral home was connected to God's ultimate ownership of the land, the demand that liberty be given to all the slaves was connected to God's ultimate ownership of all the Israelites.

IS IT PRACTICAL?

For most modern people, the very idea of a general forgiveness of debts and the inability to sell or to transfer land permanently is unthinkable. We are aware that much of our economy is maintained through borrowing and lending. If we were to simply forgive all debts and undo all land transfers, it would cause such chaos that our economy might never recover. Such considerations have led many modern people to consider the jubilee law to be quite impractical and to express doubts that it was ever actually practiced.

In fact, proclamations similar to the contents of Leviticus 25 were not that uncommon in the ancient world. In many Mesopotamian kingdoms the monarch would periodically declare a time of release when debts would be forgiven, land that had been lost would revert to its owners and debt slaves would be given their freedom.[103] Examples of such proclamations abound in the archaeological record. The Rosetta Stone is probably the most famous example. This stone, found in Egypt, was the key that permitted Egyptologists to finally decipher the hieroglyphic writing on Egypt's ancient monuments because it contained an ancient proclamation written in hieroglyphics, Demotic Egyptian and Greek. But what was the proclamation that was so famously inscribed on this stone? It was a proclamation of a debt cancellation by Pharaoh Ptolemy V made in 196 BCE.[104]

---

[102] Leviticus 25:54,55
[103] See "The Economic Roots of the Jubilee," by Michael Hudson, *Bible Review*, Ed. by Hershel Shanks. February 1999 pp. 26
[104] Ibid. p. 33.

Yes, ancient monarchs did sometimes make such proclamations. They had their reasons for doing it. They knew that their power base depended on the free men of their kingdoms who lived on their own little plots of land. These were the people who provided soldiers for their armies and who formed their tax base. The king needed these people to remain on their land and to pass their holdings down to the next generation. He made such proclamations to protect them so that they could continue to support him. There may have been powerful people in society who wanted to see many people reduced to slavery and their small fields joined together to grow cash crops, but the king's interest generally ran contrary to them. And the king made the laws.

Historically speaking, it is not surprising that Ancient Israel had a legal mechanism that allowed for the forgiving of debts, the restoration of lost property and the freeing of debt slaves. What is unique about the law that we find in Leviticus 25 is that it does not leave the imposition of such measures to the whim of the king so that he can use them at the time when it is most advantageous to him, such as when he is recruiting for a war. According to this law, the release is to take place at regular intervals following God's schedule and not the king's needs.

WAS IT PRACTICED?

The Old Testament records two occasions when a jubilee was enacted. The first is during the reign of Zedekiah:

> The word that came to Jeremiah from the LORD,
> after King Zedekiah had made a covenant with all
> the people in Jerusalem to make a proclamation of
> liberty to them—that all should set free their
> Hebrew slaves, male and female, so that no one
> should hold another Judean in slavery. And they
> obeyed, all the officials and all the people who had
> entered into the covenant that all would set free
> their slaves, male or female, so that they would not
> be enslaved again; they obeyed and set them
> free. But afterwards they turned around and took
> back the male and female slaves they had set free,
> and brought them again into subjection as slaves.[105]

---

[105] Jeremiah 34:8-11

75

This does not mention all of the elements of a Biblical jubilee and focuses primarily on the matter of freeing slaves. Even more significant, the jubilee is not proclaimed according to God's timetable as indicated in the Book of Leviticus but at a time that serves the interests of the king. It is a matter of a covenant between Zedekiah and the people. The covenant would have been sealed in the ancient manner—by slaughtering an animal, cutting it in half and then walking between the two halves.[106]

The particular interests of King Zedekiah likely had to do with the threat of war. At the time he was desperately fending off an invasion force from Babylon and he needed the freed slaves to fight in his army. What's more, the need was short lived—or at least Zedekiah and the people thought it was. For some reason, the Babylonians must have retreated or turned their attention elsewhere and the Israelites no longer felt the situation was so desperate. Once the crisis passed, the people simply took their slaves back and for this action they were soundly condemned by the prophet Jeremiah:

> Therefore, thus says the LORD: You have not
> obeyed me by granting a release to your neighbours
> and friends; I am going to grant a release to you,
> says the LORD—a release to the sword, to
> pestilence, and to famine. I will make you a horror
> to all the kingdoms of the earth. And those who
> transgressed my covenant and did not keep the
> terms of the covenant that they made before me, I
> will make like the calf when they cut it in two and
> passed between its parts: the officials of Judah, the
> officials of Jerusalem, the eunuchs, the priests, and
> all the people of the land who passed between the
> parts of the calf shall be handed over to their
> enemies and to those who seek their lives. Their
> corpses shall become food for the birds of the air
> and the wild animals of the earth. And as for King
> Zedekiah of Judah and his officials, I will hand
> them over to their enemies and to those who seek
> their lives, to the army of the king of Babylon,
> which has withdrawn from you. I am going to
> command, says the LORD, and will bring them
> back to this city; and they will fight against it, and

---

[106] Such a covenant ceremony is described in Genesis 15:9-20.

76

take it, and burn it with fire. The towns of Judah I will make a desolation without inhabitant.[107]

Jeremiah's prediction was chillingly correct for two good reasons. It was correct because the Babylonians would indeed soon return and resume their siege of Jerusalem. It was also correct for completely practical reasons. By revoking the freedom that had been given to the slaves, the king and the nobility had squandered whatever good will they had among the lower classes. These people, having been fooled once, would not soon trust the king again. Nor would they be willing to fight the next time the Babylonians came around. Zedekiah had indeed doomed his kingdom to destruction.

So the first recorded jubilee in the Bible was not a big success. The second is a much more encouraging example. This one was held during the governorship of Nehemiah. We read in the fifth chapter of the book of Nehemiah that many of the Israelites who had returned from exile and settled in Jerusalem were struggling because of the high taxes they had to pay to the king of Persia. This meant that they had to borrow money to get by. Their debts were spiralling out of control leading to the loss of their land and debt slavery. Nehemiah stepped in to correct all the wrongs at once:

> I was very angry when I heard their outcry and these complaints. After thinking it over, I brought charges against the nobles and the officials; I said to them, "You are all taking interest from your own people." And I called a great assembly to deal with them, and said to them, "As far as we were able, we have bought back our Jewish kindred who had been sold to other nations; but now you are selling your own kin, who must then be bought back by us!" They were silent, and could not find a word to say. So I said, "The thing that you are doing is not good. Should you not walk in the fear of our God, to prevent the taunts of the nations our enemies? Moreover I and my brothers and my servants are lending them money and grain. Let us stop this taking of interest. Restore to them, this very day, their fields, their vineyards, their olive orchards, and their houses, and the interest on money, grain, wine, and oil that you have been exacting from them." Then they said, "We will

---

[107] Jeremiah 34:17-22

restore everything and demand nothing more from
them. We will do as you say." …And the people
did as they had promised.[108]

Nehemiah's measures are very much like the measures found in
the jubilee law. Indeed the only thing that is really missing is the
timetable. This one does not seem to have been held 50 years after
the last one. Nehemiah is starting all over again in a city and a
nation that has been completely ruined. He doesn't really have any
historical precedents that he could use to calculate an appropriate
date for a jubilee. Nevertheless, it seems clear that Nehemiah is
motivated by God's call for justice within the society as well as a
desire to strengthen every segment of society. His call for jubilee is
not self-serving, but springs from a desire for a just distribution of
the resources of the nation. This is very much in keeping with the
spirit of the jubilee law found in Leviticus 25.

So there is evidence that the jubilee law was followed at least
twice (even if one of those times it was a failure). We cannot know
how consistently it was practiced over the years and during what
periods, but it was an economic tool that was employed even if only
imperfectly. Our assumptions that such measures would cause too
much economic chaos are rooted very much in our modern
economic system—a system that really has very little connection to
the economies of the ancient world.

THE END OF JUBILEE

Sometime between 30 BCE and 10 CE, a measure was
introduced in the Sanhedrin, the council of elders, in Jerusalem by
the famed teacher of the law, Hillel. This measure made it possible
to insert a legal clause, called a *prosbul*, into a statement of debt that
made it jubilee proof, a debt that would not be forgiven in the
sabbath year.[109] Such a measure effectively destroyed the very basis
of the jubilee law because the sabbath year and the jubilee year were
two parts of the same mechanism for restoring the balance of
wealth in the nation. Now that it was possible for creditors to offer
loans that could never be cancelled, why would they offer the other
kind ever again?

That such a legal change was enacted at that time tells us a few
things. First, Hillel would not have felt any need to introduce the

---

[108] Nehemiah 5:6 - 13
[109] Michael Hudson, op. cit. p.44.

prosbul if the sabbath year and the year of jubilee were not being observed. The mere fact that such a measure was felt to be necessary indicates that debts were still being cancelled at that date. The jubilee law was at least partially still in force, therefore, up until about the time of the birth of Christ—though, from that time forth, it essentially lost any effectiveness it once had. The introduction of the *prosbul* was the effective end of the jubilee.

The second thing that this measure tells us is that Hillel and his cohorts on the Sanhedrin were dealing with a new reality at that time. If the jubilee had endured and continued to be practiced (no doubt imperfectly but practiced nonetheless) for generations, what was different about conditions at the turn of the era that made it no longer practical?

Jewish tradition states that Hillel introduced the *prosbul* to assist the poor and needy: "For he saw that people were unwilling to lend money to one another and disregarded the precept laid down in the Torah."[110] Hillel may well have been moved by the plight of the poor in his day, but it is important to recognize that the sabbath year law and the jubilee law had *always* made the wealthy understandably reluctant to lend to the poor. This was certainly not a *new* problem at the turn of the era. There must be some other situation that made the new law necessary enough to persuade Hillel and the other elders that they had no other choice but to go against what God's law clearly stated.

I would argue that the new reality that necessitated such a change was the growing power and influence of the Roman Empire in Judea, especially the full integration of the territory into a province in 6 CE. The Romans had an economic agenda that was more ambitious than the agendas of all the empires that had preceded it. The Romans sought to boost both business and tax revenues from all of its territories by creating large-scale industries. One of the ways they did this in many of their provinces was by creating what they called *latifundia*. *Latifundia* were huge industrial farms where vast swaths of land were worked by large gangs of slaves to produce cash crops. The creation of *latifundia* required two things—the ability to join many small fields together and a large pool of slave labour. The jubilee law stood in the way of both of those things by fostering a society where free people lived on their own land. The Sanhedrin likely found itself under tremendous

---

[110] *Babylonian Talmud: Tractate Gittin*, Tr. by Rabbi Dr. I. Epstein, The Soncino Press, London, 1935-1948, Folio 36a.

pressure to find a way around this ancient religious law that was standing in the way of Roman profits.

The Sanhedrin gave in and introduced a measure that would have made it impossible for anyone who was unwilling to agree to a *prosbul* to get a loan. But the idea of jubilee would not have been forgotten, especially among those for whom it had been their only hope for any sort of economic relief.

A POWERFUL IDEAL

The big underlying assumption of the jubilee year—that every family must simply be content with subsisting on its own little plot of land—is somewhat troubling. Such an economic philosophy has a tendency to stifle such things as innovation, creativity and economic growth. It would be hard for us to imagine living today under such restrictions, though our worsening environmental situation may well lead us all to look again at the question of how much of the earth's resources each person needs to build a good life.

It is hard for us to see how a strict and absolutely consistent application of the jubilee law would have really helped the nation of Israel to reach its full economic potential. As a legal and economic measure, it was doubtlessly imperfect. Nevertheless, this law provided an enduring symbol to stand in opposition to the excesses of greed. It represented an idea to which the prophets often appealed as they sought to counter those in their society who prospered at the expense of their fellow Israelites.

When, for example, the prophet Elijah condemns King Ahab and Queen Jezebel for their scheme to confiscate the ancestral land of Naboth the Jezreelite, he does so with full assurance that God's wrath is burning hot against the king.[111] Other prophets freely condemn those wealthy Israelites who are doing things to their fellow Israelites that would be undone by a jubilee year:

> Hear this, you that trample on the needy,
> and bring to ruin the poor of the land,
> saying, "When will the new moon be over
> so that we may sell grain;
> and the sabbath,
> so that we may offer wheat for sale?
> We will make the ephah small and the shekel great,

---

[111] 1 Kings 21:17 ff.

80

and practice deceit with false balances,
buying the poor for silver
and the needy for a pair of sandals,
and selling the sweepings of the wheat."
The LORD has sworn by the pride of Jacob:
Surely I will never forget any of their deeds.[112]

Alas for those who devise wickedness
and evil deeds on their beds!
When the morning dawns, they perform it,
because it is in their power.
They covet fields, and seize them;
houses, and take them away;
they oppress householder and house,
people and their inheritance.
Therefore thus says the LORD:
Now, I am devising against this family an evil
from which you cannot remove your necks;
and you shall not walk haughtily,
for it will be an evil time.[113]

The strong rhetoric suggests that the very idea of a jubilee provided a rallying point for all those who suffered under the hand of the wealthy and powerful.

A SURPRISING PROCLAMATION

Perhaps the most astonishing pronouncement concerning the jubilee is found in the Book of Isaiah. It is in the third section of the book, in a collection of prophecies that were probably made many years after the death of the original Prophet Isaiah but that took his ideas and themes and applied them to some challenging new times. This collection is called "Third Isaiah" (or Trito-Isaiah) by many scholars, and so the anonymous prophet (or prophets) who spoke them is often called Third Isaiah for convenience. And, in the sixty-first chapter of Isaiah, Third Isaiah begins to speak on the subject of jubilee:

The spirit of the Lord GOD is upon me,
because the LORD has anointed me;
he has sent me to bring good news to the

---

[112] Amos 8:4-7
[113] Micah 2:1-3

oppressed,
to bind up the brokenhearted,
to proclaim liberty to the captives,
and release to the prisoners;
to proclaim the year of the LORD's favour,
and the day of vengeance of our God;
to comfort all who mourn;
to provide for those who mourn in Zion—
to give them a garland instead of ashes,
the oil of gladness instead of mourning,
the mantle of praise instead of a faint spirit.[114]

The prophet here takes up all of the language of the jubilee proclamation, although he doesn't actually use the word. When he promises such things as "good news for the oppressed, …liberty …and release," he is talking about the kinds of things that a jubilee was supposed to accomplish. The surprising thing is that the prophet actually takes it upon himself—not as someone who has any sort of worldly authority but merely as someone who has the "Spirit of the Lord GOD" upon him—to declare that the jubilee year has arrived. It would seem that Third Isaiah looked around and saw many wrongs within his society. He decided that things had gotten so bad that a jubilee was desperately needed, and so he declared that it had come.

This is, when you think about it, a deliciously subversive idea. If all you need to instigate a jubilee is to have the spirit of the Lord God come upon you, then really it is something that anyone can do. Or, to be more precise, it is something that God can use anyone to do.

This is another step in the idea of jubilee. It started out as a commonly accepted year of release in many Near Eastern societies that could be proclaimed by the king at a time and in a way that served his own needs and interests. It became, in the Book of Leviticus, something that was held on a regular schedule as mandated by God and not the king. But here, in the Book of Isaiah, it has become something that a prophet of God can call at any time based on the needs of the people and despite the fact that it might be totally inconvenient to king and creditors alike.

The big problem with this proclamation of jubilee in the Book of Isaiah is compliance. After all, just because Third Isaiah declares that God says that it's time for a jubilee doesn't mean that key

---

[114] Isaiah 61:1-3

people such as creditors or political authorities will agree. Indeed, in all likelihood, such people laughed at the very idea that they should release their slaves and return land that they had seized or purchased because Third Isaiah said so. It would take a competent political power to force them to do what was against their own economic interests. The poor, the dispossessed and the slaves, on the other hand, would have received Third Isaiah's proclamation with joy and enthusiasm.

What would be the point in calling a jubilee if nobody who could free slaves, return land or forgive debts responded? Why bother? I suspect that Third Isaiah knew what he was doing. He was invoking the symbolic power of the jubilee. He was holding it up as a rallying point for the enslaved and dispossessed and giving them hope. He was reminding them that God heard their grievances. He was giving the wealthy an opportunity to think about what they were doing to their fellow Israelites. He was giving those who did have the power to make a proclamation of a jubilee year the chance to consider what their responsibilities were.

There could be many good reasons why someone who had no power to enforce a jubilee might choose to proclaim one anyway. There would be some, particularly the downtrodden and disposed, who would respond to such a call with enthusiasm. This is an idea that we must keep in mind as we turn back to the Gospel of Luke.

INTERLUDE: A CONVERSATION ON THE WAY

As the two expectant parents travel down the road side by side, they have a lot of time to talk. Mary is very young and doesn't know much about the world. All her life she has lived in the small village of Nazareth. Joseph is also from the same area, but she knows that his family has not been settled there nearly so long as her own.

People in small villages like Nazareth have long memories. They do not easily accept new people into their community—not even those who have been there for many generations. It is why the people there still talk about how, a generation ago, Joseph's family arrived as refugees from Judea.

The family has never talked much about what had happened to them before they resettled as landless artisans in the small Galilean village. But there is plenty of time to talk now as Mary and Joseph make their slow progress down the road.

"Husband," asks Mary. "You told those soldiers that we are heading for Bethlehem. Is that the place that your family came from?"

"Yes, indeed," Joseph replies. "Though I have never been there, I cannot wait to see it. All my life my parents and grandparents have told me of the home that we had there. They described to me the house, the garden and the field, so often that I can imagine the place down to the last detail. I know that I've always lived in Galilee, but I cannot help but feel as if Bethlehem is my true home."

"You must have had a large and beautiful house there."

"No, no greater than any family holding in Nazareth, though my father says that the land was good. It always produced an abundant barley crop."

"I suppose that is why they call the town 'Beth Lehem,'"[115] Mary interjects, "because it is a good place for growing grain."

"Yes, but you don't get rich growing barley, do you? Our people certainly never did. I know that some people in Nazareth say that my family comes from the house and lineage of King David. Don't deny it! I have heard the people talking around town! The rumour may well be true, but, if it is, it hardly means that our ancestors were wealthy. According to the lore of my family we are not descended from a long line of kings. We come from the more humble branch of the family. My forefathers did not go to sit on thrones in Jerusalem. They were the ones who stayed behind in Bethlehem and continued to live on the land that once belonged to Jesse, David's father and before him had belonged Obed and then to Boaz."

"Boaz! But doesn't that mean that your family farm is the very same place where Ruth, the Moabitess, came to Boaz while he was in his tent and they..."[116] Mary blushes and falls silent.

"Well, that's the story that we tell in my family," Joseph laughs. "It's one of the reasons why the land is so special to us. But, apart from its place in the history of our people, the land was not remarkable. The only land that we ever had in Bethlehem was the same little plot of land that God gave to each Israelite family and we love the place not because it is rich or grand but simply because it is ours."

"They won't give it back to you, you know."

"I know," Joseph sighs. "But that doesn't change the fact that it is ours. God gave it to our family and it is God's will that it stay in our family until the Day of the Lord may come."

Mary walks on in silence for a while. A lovely little valley opens up ahead and to the left of their path. She

---

[115] Hebrew: House of bread.
[116] Ruth 3,4

sees a small homestead in the valley. There is only about an acre of land but every inch of it seems to be used to grow something. There is a fig tree and two olive trees. In one corner she can see a cluster of vines. The grapes are still green but she knows that they will ripen soon. In the middle of the field, the peasant struggles to break up the ground with his simple plough so that he can sow some grain. He does not have an animal to pull the plough and so he must scrape the land himself with the help of a small boy who is probably his son.

Joseph's family's land must have looked something like this. Mary imagines what it would be for her to live with her husband and with her own son in such a place. It would not be an easy life. The work would be hard and the outcomes would never be guaranteed. But at least it would be a little bit more secure than living from one carpentry job to the next. She realizes that the quest that they are on is as much the fulfilment of her own dreams as it is of Joseph's and she understands the longing for a piece of land to call his own that she hears in his voice.

She just has to ask: "How did your family lose the land?"

"In the usual way," Joseph sighs. "They got into debt and couldn't get out. We blame King Herod, of course."

Mary nods. All the people that she knows have their own reasons to remember Herod and his policies with scorn.

Joseph continues, "He raised taxes to try and keep the emperor happy after he ended up on the wrong side of the civil war. My family was left with nothing at all to live on. They were starving. And so, when a creditor came along and offered a loan, what choice did they have? Of course, he insisted that there be a *prosbul* and they were in no position to refuse. The debt could never be forgiven.

"The interest rate was very high and they soon fell behind in their payments. With no hope of relief, it was inevitable. They lost the land. It's the same thing that has happened to thousands of Judean families. Mine is no different."

"But now we are returning there," Mary says with a hint of fear in her voice. "What will happen when we arrive?"

"We shall see," says Joseph. "We shall see."

They have now come up to the entrance to the small homestead that Mary had seen and at Joseph's suggestion they turn aside to speak with the farmer. Joseph offers to make some repairs to the man's farm implements in exchange for a meal. The farmer agrees gladly and Joseph takes out his simple carpentry tools and gets to work. Afterwards, Mary and Joseph join the small family for a simple but wholesome meal. In accordance with the ancient laws of hospitality, the family also offers them a safe place to lay down their belongings on this night.

They eat well and sleep in safety for a change. And in the morning they will continue on towards Bethlehem and whatever trouble awaits them there.

Jesus came to announce the arrival of something that he called the kingdom of God (or, in Matthew's Gospel, the kingdom of heaven).[117] While the kingdom of God was certainly not the same thing as the year of jubilee, the two concepts seem to have shared certain concerns and goals.

The kingdom that Jesus announced belonged to the poor, for example, while the rich were condemned because they had already received their consolation.[118] Jesus also spent a great deal of time, in his parables about the kingdom and in other sayings, talking about debts and how they needed to be forgiven—sharing the same concern that lies behind the jubilee law. He even incorporated the need for financial relief into the famous prayer that he taught to his disciples.

> And forgive us our debts,
> as we also have forgiven our debtors.[119]

Of course, in many cases he seems to have used the idea of forgiving financial debts as a metaphor for the forgiveness of sins— a kind of spiritual debt that we owe to God or to the people that we have wronged. But the fact that Jesus consistently chose to use the word debt when talking about such matters is surely significant. He carried out his ministry at a time when the Roman economic program was transforming the social landscape of Galilee and when people were losing their ancestral lands due to high taxes and mounting debts. When Jesus spoke about debts, the people— particularly the poor who seemed to form the core of his following (the people to whom he said "Blessed are you who are poor, for yours is the kingdom of God.")[120]—could not have failed to make some connections to their own financial woes even if they did also think about their spiritual needs.

Jesus shows a particular concern in his stories and sayings for those who do not have any land. His parables make frequent mention of slaves, day labourers and tenant farmers.[121] These were

---

[117] See Mark 1:15, Matthew 4:7
[118] Luke 6:20,24
[119] Matthew 6:11
[120] Luke 6:20
[121] E.g. Luke 12:23-48; Matthew 20:1-16; Mark 12:1-12.

all people whose lack of land ownership put them at an extreme disadvantage in that economy. The parables are often told from the vantage point of these people and deal with their concerns.

Jesus himself is identified, with a certain amount of derision, as a carpenter and a carpenter's son:

> They said, "Where did this man get all this? What
> is this wisdom that has been given to him? What
> deeds of power are being done by his hands! Is not
> this the carpenter, the son of Mary…?" And they
> took offense at him.[122]

This may be a bit confusing for us because we tend to see carpenters as skilled artisans or tradespeople and assume that it is possible for them to prosper handsomely from their work. This kind of thing did not happen in first century Galilee. Carpenters, for them, were people who were severely disadvantaged because they did not own any agricultural land. They were often former farmers who had lost or failed to inherit their ancestral land.[123] They may have been better off than those who ended up as slaves, tenant farmers or day labours because they had access to certain skills and tools and this would have given them some advantages, but they would still have been counted among the dispossessed.

There cannot have been much paying work for a carpenter in a small village like Nazareth. Perhaps Joseph and even Jesus himself could have gotten occasional work in the city of Sepphoris which was only three or four miles away and was being built up throughout most of the time of Jesus's childhood, but even that would likely have only been on a day-labour basis and it would have offered little economic stability to Joseph's family.

Jesus likely would have counted himself among the landless of Galilee and so it is certainly not surprising that there is a certain implicit support for the ideals of the jubilee in his teachings. Whatever is implicit elsewhere, Luke makes quite explicit in his gospel, for he makes the year of jubilee a major theme. In a key episode, when Jesus inaugurates his public ministry at Nazareth, Luke tells us that he is handed the scroll of Isaiah and reads the jubilee proclamation passage from Isaiah 61.

---

[122] Mark 6:2,3. See also Matthew 13:55.
[123] See John Dominic Crossan, *The Historical Jesus*, HarperSanFrancisco, 1992, pp. 45,46.

"The Spirit of the Lord is upon me,
because he has anointed me
to bring good news to the poor.
He has sent me to proclaim release to the captives
and recovery of sight to the blind,
to let the oppressed go free,
to proclaim the year of the Lord's favour."[124]

He then sits down and calmly announces, "Today this scripture has been fulfilled in your hearing."[125] In other words, Jesus is announcing that the jubilee year has begun, presumably because he has arrived.

This passage is very important because Luke uses it to introduce the themes that he will highlight throughout the rest of this gospel. It is similar to the following passage at the beginning of the Book of Acts:

But you will receive power when the Holy Spirit
has come upon you; and you will be my witnesses
in Jerusalem, in all Judea and Samaria, and to the
ends of the earth."[126]

In that verse, Luke literally maps out the story he will tell throughout the rest of the Book of Acts, tracing the spread of the gospel from Jerusalem to the rest of Judea, to Samaria and finally, with the preaching of Paul, to the ends of the known earth. In the same way, with Jesus's inaugural sermon at Nazareth, Luke maps out the future course of his gospel telling us as it begins what Jesus's ministry will accomplish. Luke is declaring that, at least in part, he will understand and interpret Jesus's ministry through the lens of the year of jubilee.

He certainly follows through on that promise. Throughout the rest of his gospel, Luke consistently highlights ideas and images that are related to the jubilee. You can see this particularly in the material that, like his nativity story, is unique to Luke's gospel. Luke includes a number of parables that are not recounted in the other gospels and almost all of them touch on jubilee themes.

---

[124] Luke 4:18,19
[125] Luke 4:21
[126] Acts 1:8

The parable of the Rich Fool (Luke 12:13-21), for example, is provoked by a request regarding the inheritance of property: "Teacher, tell my brother to divide the family inheritance with me."[127] It is also sharply critical of those who are greedy and who collect an abundance of possessions for themselves—more than they need to sustain their life. It ends with God condemning the rich man and taking steps to restore a more equal ownership in society. "You fool!" God says, "This very night your life is being demanded of you. And the things you have prepared, whose will they be?"[128] Such as radical redistribution of wealth and property was also supposed to be what God accomplished through the year of jubilee.

THE PRODIGAL SON

Luke is the only evangelist to record Jesus's parable of the Prodigal Son (Luke 15:11-32). This parable is also concerned with a matter of the inheritance of property. The circumstances of the story seem to arise from the high degree of uncertainty around inheritance in the first century.

Both the father and the 'prodigal' son behave in ways that do not make sense under normal circumstances. Normally a son would not even dream of asking his father to give him his inheritance before his father dies and yet that is what this son does. Even stranger is the father's willingness to agree to his son's demand. What could possibly motivate a father to do something so contrary to the normal practise as to pass on to one of his sons his entire inheritance so long before his own death?

If we understand that many first century families were living in the fear that they would lose their ancestral properties, however, the actions of both father and son make a perverse kind of sense. If he has reason to believe that his family's property will be gone by the time he comes to inherit, then a son might well feel that he is justified to ask for it ahead of time. At least then he might be able to get a little enjoyment out of it before it is gone forever. In the same way, a father who is afraid that taxes and debts will push him out of his ancestral home before he has a chance to give anything to his children might well be desperate enough to give his son his heritage early in order to be able to at least give him something. Under normal circumstances, the behaviour of both father and son would

---

[127] Luke 12:13
[128] Luke 12:20

make little sense. It would seem that Roman policies in the first century had created economic circumstances for families that were anything but normal.

In this parable, Jesus seems to be portraying fellow Judeans or Galileans who are dealing with the same kinds of economic problems that we know were present in the early first century. Something has gone wrong in the system of inheritance and this has created a crisis in the relationship between the generations.

If that is the crisis, then it is interesting to note that the parable proposes a solution to the crisis that comes in the form of a sort of jubilee. At the climax of the story the lost son makes a journey back to his ancestral home which no longer legally belongs to him. When he arrives, he submits himself as a slave to his father but is given release from that slavery and received as a son instead. This story contains the essential jubilee elements of *return* to the ancestral property and *release* from slavery. It is a jubilee story.

THE UNJUST STEWARD

Immediately after the Prodigal Son, Luke includes his unique parable of the Unjust Steward (Luke 16:1-13). In this parable, Jesus praises a steward who forgives the debts that are owed to his master even though the man does so without his master's knowledge. People have long puzzled over Jesus's praise of this duplicitous steward. The story makes more sense if we understand that the forgiveness of debts, which was integral to the observance of jubilee, was considered to be a matter of obedience to God's commands. This parable suggests that such forgiveness is admirable even if it takes place behind the back of the lender!

The parable of the Unjust Steward also provokes a unique response from the Pharisees who are listening to Jesus in Luke's gospel:

> The Pharisees, who were lovers of money, heard all
> this, and they ridiculed him. So he said to them,
> "You are those who justify yourselves in the sight
> of others; but God knows your hearts; for what is
> prized by human beings is an abomination in the
> sight of God."[129]

Could this sharp criticism of the Pharisees as money lovers have something to do with their support of Hillel's *prosbul* legislation

---

[129] Luke 16:14-15

which had the effect of preventing debts from being forgiven during the sabbath year? Hillel was certainly highly esteemed by the Pharisees and so they might well have been closely associated with this legislative effort. It is interesting to speculate that this legislation, which could well have been regarded by some as "an abomination in the sight of God," might have still been a point of controversy during Jesus's lifetime and even when this gospel was written a century or more after the death of Hillel.

It seems clear that Luke, in the material that he chooses to include in his gospel, is going out of his way to present Jesus's ministry as being a proclamation of the arrival of the jubilee. Since Jesus's ministry almost certainly lasted more than one year, Luke is not thinking of a jubilee that is limited only to such a length of time. He is rather talking about the jubilee as a symbol that is only limited by God's grace and not human calendars.

But is this jubilee theme truly introduced only in the fourth chapter of Luke and limited to the public ministry of Jesus, or does Luke see it as something that began even before Jesus stood to speak in the Nazareth synagogue?

THE JUBILEE IN THE NATIVITY STORY

As I have already suggested, the census that is described in the second chapter of the Gospel of Luke is problematic. Although the Romans were indeed very keen on taking censuses and did take a major inaugural census of Judea in 6 CE, they did not require people to return to their ancestral homes to be registered. Indeed, such a mass migration of people would likely do more to disrupt the process and render any results useless. The Romans would have been foolish to conduct a census in such a manner and there is no evidence that they ever did so.

If we can find no precedent in Roman law or practice for such a requirement, why is it present in Luke's story? If it is not a common Roman practice, where else could it come from? We have already noted the tendency of the New Testament writers to look to Old Testament passages to fill the holes and make sense of their narratives. Luke may well have sought such inspiration at this point in his account. There is only one Old Testament passage that speaks of the requirement of all the people to return to their ancestral homes and that is the jubilee law of Leviticus 25. Perhaps Luke has this law in mind as he writes.

Look again at the familiar passage in which Luke describes the political and social situation at the time of the birth of Jesus.

> In those days a decree went out from Emperor Augustus that all the world should be registered. This was the first registration and was taken while Quirinius was governor of Syria. All went to their own towns to be registered. Joseph also went from the town of Nazareth in Galilee to Judea, to the city of David called Bethlehem, because he was descended from the house and family of David. He went to be registered with Mary, to whom he was engaged and who was expecting a child.[130]

Luke states only that Caesar Augustus required that all the people be registered. This is undoubtedly true as any census would have been taken under the authority of the emperor even though he would not have personally issued the specific decrees. He then says that "All went to their own towns to be registered." But, significantly, he does not say that Caesar told them to do that. Is it possible that Luke is saying that a year of jubilee was held at the same time that the Romans were holding their census and that all went to their ancestral homes, not because of the census, but because of the jubilee?

Such an idea would certainly help Luke to solve certain logistical problems in his narrative. Luke says that Mary and Joseph are from the small village of Nazareth.[131] He must explain how a couple from Nazareth happened to be in Bethlehem when their son was born. The Roman census, although it is useful in making other important points, cannot explain that, because a census demanded no such travel. Only a jubilee could account for the kind of travel that Luke talks about.

Introducing the idea of jubilee into the nativity account also helps Luke make some important theological points. It allows him to associate the idea of jubilee with the entire life and ministry of Jesus—to say that the jubilee "year" began with Jesus's birth and continued to be proclaimed and to grow throughout his whole life.

The idea also makes it clear that Jesus's birth took place, not only under the imperial authority of Rome, but also under the benevolent authority of God. It may be up to Caesar to decide when

---

[130] Luke 2:1-5
[131] Luke 2:39

a census should be taken but it is up to God to say when it is time for jubilee. It makes the point that Mary and Joseph's journey to Bethlehem was made in obedience to God and not to Rome.

The jubilee journey also reinforces Luke's theological point that Jesus was born into poverty for, under the jubilee law, only those who have lost their ancestral lands because of poverty should have to return to that land from any great distance. If Joseph's journey from Nazareth to Bethlehem is, indeed, a jubilee homecoming journey, then it marks Joseph as one of the many dispossessed people of early first century Palestine.

A jubilee held at the same time would also solve a few other problems with Luke's narrative. Even if (as seems extremely unlikely) the census that was held in 6 CE obliged the people of Judea and Samaria to return to their ancestral homes, that would not explain why Joseph, residing in Galilee, should travel to Bethlehem because Galileans were not included in the census. It only applied to Judeans and Samaritans who were, at that time, becoming a part of the Roman world. The census was limited to the borders of these territories and that meant that Joseph had no obligation to be registered. But a call to jubilee knew no borders. If a jubilee were proclaimed, all Jews would be obliged to respond no matter what territory they lived in. Joseph might not be under Rome's direct rule but, as a Jew, he would certainly see himself as being under God's.

In the same way, while the census would have imposed no obligation for Mary to travel to Bethlehem because women did not count in a census, the call to jubilee would have applied to her because, as a wife, she would participate in the claim to Joseph's ancestral property. She did not need to travel to please Rome but she would joyfully travel, despite the danger, in order to please God.

PROBLEMS WITH THIS PROPOSAL

There are certain problems with the notion of seeing a jubilee celebration in what Luke is describing in this passage. For one thing, he cannot be describing a fully observed jubilee. There is no sense in which, when Joseph returns to Bethlehem, the ancestral land to which he has a claim is restored to him. On the contrary, when he arrives in the town there is no place for him and his wife to stay, despite their extreme circumstances. Luke gives no indication that anyone else is given back their land either and no slaves are freed. The only elements of a Biblical jubilee that we can detect are the (presumed) proclamation and the mass return of people to their ancestral homes.

As we have seen in Third Isaiah's proclamation of the jubilee year in Isaiah 61, it was possible for prophets who had the Spirit of the Lord upon them to make a proclamation of jubilee even if they had no power or authority to make the big landholders and slave-owners actually offer release. Such a call would have been welcomed by the poor and embraced by many as a kind of peaceful protest against the kinds of things that were going on throughout the Judean countryside.

We know that the census of 6 CE and the new taxes associated with it did cause considerable opposition. The Roman tax system in the provinces was notoriously corrupt and the cause of much misery as the publicans squeezed every penny they could out of the populace. It was one of the tools that the Romans used to dispossess people of their land and push them into poverty and slavery so that Italian businessmen could come along and create large industrial farms that were worked by large gangs of slaves. The common people hated the tax collectors and all they represented and so the census, being taken to create better tax rolls, gave them a unique opportunity to show their displeasure.

One of the ways that they could have shown their displeasure would have been by calling a jubilee. This would have led to a mass displacement of people as they returned to their ancestral homes. With so many people being registered in places other than where they resided, the census would have generated tax rolls that were of little practical use to the tax collectors. It is admittedly a rather passive-aggressive way of protesting against the Roman tax system, but many Jews would have felt that it was the only kind of protest they could afford to make. Perhaps even Galilean Jews might have been willing to participate in this disruption in hopes of deepening Roman aggravation.

The biggest problem with this proposal for reading Luke's birth narrative is that it is so obscure. If Luke wants to make the point that the birth of Jesus was a jubilee event, why doesn't he say so much more clearly? Luke, like all the gospel writers, has to be very careful about some of the things he says. He cannot write anything that is too overtly critical of the Roman Empire and he certainly does not dare to include openly anything that might portray Jesus or his parents as rebels.

We can see this particularly in the way that Luke and all the gospel writers portray the execution of Jesus. Jesus was obviously executed by Roman authorities because he was put to death using the uniquely Roman method of crucifixion. Nevertheless, the evangelists go out of their way in their accounts of the trials and the death of Jesus to shift as much of the blame as they can from Pilate and the Roman administration to the Jewish authorities and, sometimes, to the entire Jewish people. They are doing this to help ensure the survival of the church, to reassure the Romans in the aftermath of the Jewish Rebellion of 66-70 CE that the Christian church will not disturb the *pax romanum*—the Roman peace.

Luke is naturally cautious about saying too openly that Jesus's parents participated in an action that may have been intended to disrupt the census. He tells the story in such a way that an outsider would not have detected anything amiss (though they might have been puzzled by Luke's description of the census). But to those who were in the church, I am not so sure that the reference would have been so obscure.

The earliest Christians were quite accustomed to searching through many kinds of Old Testament literature to understand the events of Jesus's life. Being familiar with the Roman way of taking censuses, they would have immediately seen something in Luke's account that didn't make much sense and they would have naturally searched through the scriptures for a solution to the problem. When they saw that Joseph was making a journey towards his ancestral home in Bethlehem and they would have remembered the Biblical promise that he should own property there, they would have noticed that he had no place to stay when he went there. This would have put them in mind of the jubilee law that would have remedied such a situation. I believe that Luke left enough clues in his account to lead the insiders of the church to the conclusion he wanted them to make. After searching the scriptures, it is quite possible that they would have seen that the only way to understand Joseph's journey was as a part of a jubilee.

"NO PLACE FOR THEM IN THE INN"

There may be another clue in the account. Bible translators have long struggled with one particular word in the nativity story. The word is most commonly translated as "inn," as in, for example, the New Revised Standard Version: "she... laid him in a manger, because there was no place for them in the *inn*."[132] The Greek word

---

[132] Luke 2:7, emphasis added.

that Luke uses in this verse is *katalyma*. The word literally means a place where a traveler lays down his baggage while on a journey but it certainly does not need to refer to the kind of commercial establishment that we would identify as an inn today. It could just as easily refer to a private home or a room within a private house where a traveler might stay. This has led Brown, among others, to suggest that the best translation of the word might be something generic like "lodging place."[133]

This was, after all, a simpler world—a world where travellers and pilgrims could expect to receive hospitality even from complete strangers. There seems to have been a very strong sense throughout the ancient Mediterranean world that there was a moral obligation for people from every level of society to be generous in offering hospitality to all travellers. Many ancient religions in the region told stories, myths and legends in which the protagonists welcomed strange travellers only to discover that they were, in fact, gods in disguise.[134] Jews also worked under the same assumption. In the Letter to the Hebrews, the writer is able to offer this encouragement to early Christians confident that they would understand his reference: "Do not neglect to show hospitality to strangers, for by doing that some have entertained angels without knowing it."[135]

It seems very likely, therefore, that, when Luke uses the word *katalyma*, he is thinking in terms of accommodations for the couple within a private home. The only thing that prevents such an interpretation is his puzzling use of the definite article. Why does he say "there was no place for them in *the* lodging place" when it might make more sense to say "there was no place for them in *any* lodging place" or something to that effect? His use of the definite article implies that his readers should know which house or room or inn in all the town of Bethlehem he is talking about.

Perhaps this is why the translation *"inn"* has been the most popular. If there was only one inn in Bethlehem that was well known to Luke's readers, that would justify Luke calling it *"the* inn." The problem with that is that Bethlehem really was a small town of little significance apart from being the birthplace of King David. It is very unlikely that such a place would have even had an inn, much less one so famous that Luke could assume that his readers would know exactly the place he was talking about.

---

[133] See Brown, pp. 399, 400.

[134] The best known example would be the myth of Baucis and Philemon, an elderly couple who entertained the gods Zeus and Hermes.

[135] Hebrews 13:2. This is likely a reference to Genesis 18:1-7.

If Joseph is truly intended to be on a jubilee journey in this passage, and if Luke's primary readers understand that, then the use of the definite article makes much more sense. If Joseph is making the journey that is prescribed in Leviticus 25, a return to his own ancestral property, then he is indeed travelling to a very particular house—the one which should be returned to him under the jubilee law. Luke seems to be making the point rather forcefully that, not only was Joseph not given back *the* house that should have been his in a jubilee year, he was also denied even temporary lodging in *that* house despite the extreme need of his wife who was about to deliver her child.

Every Christmas pageant I have ever seen suggests that the reason why there was no room in the "inn" (which is assumed, of course, to be a commercial establishment) had to do with the large number of people who were in town for the census. But that really makes no sense in the context. Luke's account never implies that there were vast numbers of people going to Bethlehem to be registered. Instead, he says that people headed off towards a great variety of destinations: "All went to their own towns to be registered."[136] There is no reason to think, based on this account, that Bethlehem should be any more or less inundated with travelers than any other town or village.

The lack of room for the newborn baby takes on new meaning—deep theological meaning—when we understand the link to Joseph's claim to ancestral property that a jubilee is supposed to enforce. It is not an indication of a lack of hotel capacity in a bustling town, but, rather, an indication of a lack of the economic justice and compassion that the Bible demanded. Luke feels that it is deeply significant that Joseph and his wife were denied even the hospitality that should have been extended to any stranger in *the* house that should properly have been his in God's eyes.

A MODEST PROPOSAL

I believe that I am on fairly firm ground, therefore, when I say that, in his account of the birth of Jesus, Luke is intentionally blending together a historical event—the census taken while Quirinius was governor—with an Old Testament concept—the year of jubilee. Most scholars already accept that the jubilee is a major theme in Luke's Gospel, but only seem to think that this theme

---

[136] Luke 2:3

begins in chapter four. I suggest that the theme actually begins in chapter two. Luke primarily introduces the jubilee into his birth narrative in order to make important theological points about who Jesus is and what his birth means. Many of these points are repeated and amplified throughout the rest of the Gospel. It might be helpful now to summarize some of the theological points that he is making.

- The arrival of Jesus in this world proclaims God's jubilee—a message of hope, healing and good news for all who are oppressed. Jesus goes on to announce this very thing at the beginning of his public ministry. (Luke 4:16–22)
- Although the power of Caesar is so great that he can bend the entire world to his will, God's power is even greater. Caesar may have his plans, but God's plans are deeper and more effective. This idea is particularly reflected and developed in the prayer of the apostles in Acts 4:23-31.
- Although Mary and Joseph give outward obedience to Caesar and his commands, they give deeper obedience to the commands of God. Service to Caesar and obedience to his commands as opposed to the commands of God is raised again in Luke 20:20-26.
- Jesus's family was poor. They were among the many in Judea who had been dispossessed of their heritage. This is reflected throughout the gospel as Jesus directs much of his preaching and ministry to the poor, calling them blessed by God. (Luke 6:20ff)

These theological truths are what are important to Luke and that is why I believe that it is so important to recover the jubilee aspect of the story so we may fully appreciate them.

It is important to say that Luke's introduction of the idea of jubilee into his story does not necessarily mean that he has any particular information that such a jubilee was proclaimed or embraced by anyone when Jesus was born. For Luke, it would have been enough for him to know that such a notion was present in an Old Testament passage that he believed referred to Jesus to justify him including it in his nativity story.

But at this point I cannot help but speculate a little bit. What if Luke does know something more about events that really took place at the time of the census? What if he knows that there really was some kind of jubilee held at that time? If we look very closely at the political, economic and social situation in Judea and Galilee in 6 CE, will we find any evidence of the observance of a jubilee similar to what Luke has in mind in his birth account? I simply cannot resist taking the next step and speculating about a jubilee that actually could have taken place around 6 CE.

After a seemingly unending journey, Mary and Joseph finally arrive in Bethlehem. Though he has never been here before, Joseph has little trouble finding his way to the small piece of land that once belonged to his family. It is exactly as his parents described it to him. He even recognizes the remains of his family's mark carved into the trunk of the fig tree that stands by the road.

He leads Mary up to the door and pauses before knocking. He hears voices inside. The master of the house is there. The man does not actually live in the house, of course. It is normally occupied by poor tenant farmers. The master has many different properties that he manages. He only happens to be here today to receive his generous portion from the grain harvest. Joseph takes the presence of the man as a sign from God. At least his case will be heard.

He knocks and in a few moments a slave comes to the door. He evaluates Joseph and his wife behind him with a glance.

"The master will give no alms today," he says. "Move along."

"I seek no alms," replies Joseph, "but have only come to claim what is mine. I am Joseph, the son of Heli, the son of Matthat. This property is my own. It has belonged to my family since it was given by God in the days of Joshua.

"Tell your master that it is God's jubilee. It is the time when he must return it to its rightful owners. On behalf of my family I have come to state our claim. It is a matter of justice and it is God's will."

What Joseph doesn't say, of course, is that he has already registered in the census, claiming the land as his own possession. It will probably be best if he and Mary are well away before the master learns of that.

With a sour look, but without a word, the slave closes the door. As Joseph listens he hears a low conversation within and a sudden burst of laughter. Before long the door opens and Joseph looks up again at the sour face of the slave.

"You're to move along. The master does not recognize your claim."

Joseph slowly nods. He had expected nothing less. As the slave turns to go, he reaches out and puts his hand on the man's shoulder. "It is as I thought. He knows nothing of God's justice, but perhaps he does know something of God's compassion."

Joseph turns and indicates Mary behind him. "It is my wife. As you can surely see, she will be having her baby very soon. He may deny his obligations according to the law of the jubilee, but surely your master will not forsake his duty to offer hospitality to travelers. Perhaps he will find it in his heart to grant us temporary lodging in a room of the house—the house that should be my own—even if it is just until the child is born."

Joseph thinks he detects a certain softening on the face of the man as he closes the door and turns again to speak to the master. But soon an even louder peal of laughter comes from the house.

"It's hospitality that he wants then, is it?" laughs the master. "Tell him that I can be generous. He may lay his brat in the feeding trough out in the field."

Joseph doesn't wait for the slave to return this time. He and Mary simply move away from the door. They go around the house and deep into the field to find the place where they will lay their child. They soon find the manger. It is roughly carved out of stone and Joseph's mind rests for a moment on the thought that it was likely carved many years ago by his own distant ancestor. There is no straw in it for the land no longer has any livestock but it is easily filled with some of the overgrown grass nearby.

They lay down their belongings and set up camp. When the child is born, they will lay him in the old feeding trough and they will take comfort in the act. For at least they will know that their child has been born on that piece of land that God gave to Joseph's family to be their possession forever.

Who knows, perhaps even in the cruelty and twisted sense of humour of the master, God has a plan.

6) Two Nonviolent Insurgencies

A few chapters ago we took a look at that odd passage in the Book of Acts where Luke reports on a secret conversation held in the Sanhedrin. Gamaliel, the famous rabbi, whom Luke reveres as the teacher of Paul,[137] gives a speech in which he compares and contrasts Jesus of Nazareth with two rebels.

> "Fellow Israelites, consider carefully what you
> propose to do to these men. For some time ago
> Theudas rose up, claiming to be somebody, and a
> number of men, about four hundred, joined him;
> but he was killed, and all who followed him were
> dispersed and disappeared. After him Judas the
> Galilean rose up at the time of the census and got
> people to follow him; he also perished, and all who
> followed him were scattered. So in the present
> case, I tell you, keep away from these men and let
> them alone; because if this plan or this undertaking
> is of human origin, it will fail; but if it is of God,
> you will not be able to overthrow them—in that
> case you may even be found fighting against God!"[138]

We have already seen how this passage appears to confirm that Luke is thinking that the birth of Jesus took place during "the census" of 6 CE. We have also noted that Luke, leaning as he must be on the inspiration of the Holy Spirit, is not merely reporting on what was actually said by Gamaliel but rather on his understanding of the meaning and implications of the Sanhedrin's discussion.

There is another issue in this passage that we must address. Luke seems to place the three men that Gamaliel is talking about in chronological order: Theudas, Judas and then Jesus. The mention of Theudas is problematic and it raises a few questions about Luke's sense and use of history.

Josephus, in his *Antiquities of the Jews*, does, indeed, describe the revolt of a rebel named Theudas who seems to be the man to whom Luke is referring. But that Theudas's rebellion did not come before Judas the Galilean's as it says here in Acts. According to Josephus, Theudas led his uprising about four decades *after* Judas, after the

---

[137] Acts 22:3
[138] Acts 5:35-39

time of Jesus and indeed several years after the death of Gamaliel, the elder who Luke says is speaking in this passage!

Luke seems to have his chronology quite wrong when it comes to Theudas. Most commentators who have looked closely at this passage have come to one of two conclusions. One possibility is that Luke is totally confused and has misread his historical sources here. This, to me, seems unlikely as Luke generally has a very good sense of history and does not usually depart from a straightforward recounting of events *unless it helps him make an important theological point*. The other possibility is that Luke is talking about a completely different Theudas from Josephus—a Theudas who is otherwise quite unknown to history and who lived and died sometime before the rebellion of Judas the Galilean.[139] This is a possibility, especially because Luke's account of Theudas's career seems to contradict, to a certain extent, what Josephus has to say about him.[140]

I would like to propose a third possible reading. Perhaps Luke is talking about the same Theudas as Josephus and is aware of the chronological difficulties, but has another reason to present these three men in this particular order. As I have suggested before, Luke, like the other gospel writers, is quite happy to depart from a strict recounting of the historical events when it helps him get his message across most forcefully. I suspect, therefore, that Luke sees a certain commonality between Theudas, Judas and Jesus and that there is a certain theological meaning for him in placing them in this particular order. It is why he puts them in this order despite the fact that it creates an historical error.

What is the theological message? I see two possibilities. Luke could be using these words of Gamaliel to say that there is an essential difference between Theudas and Judas on the one hand and Jesus on the other. The followers of the first two melted away when the leaders were killed which proves that God was not in those movements. Luke knows that the followers of Jesus will not melt away which proves that God is in this new Christian movement.

That is one way to interpret this passage. But, since Luke is making his point by using the voice of another person, and a purported enemy of the faith, he cannot make his meaning entirely clear. Gamaliel, in his speech, seems to be expressing contempt for

---

[139] This argument is made, e.g. by F.F. Bruce, *The Acts of the Apostles*, William B. Eerdmans Publishing Co., 1990. pp.175, 176.

[140] According to Josephus, Theudas's followers did not merely disperse as Luke says but were almost all killed by the Romans.

the movements of Theudas and Judas while he leaves open the possibility that God may be behind the Jesus movement. But that does not necessarily mean that Luke shares that sense of contempt regarding Theudas and Judas.

Perhaps, instead, Luke sees the progression of Theudas-Judas-Jesus as part of one overarching movement—a larger plan on God's part. Theudas was part of this movement and the authorities thought that they had curtailed it when Theudas died and his followers dispersed. But it sprang up again, even more powerfully in the movement of Judas the Galilean. The authorities dealt with that too. But now, Luke says through Gamaliel, it is back in a purer and more powerful form in the Christian movement. This time the authorities will never put out the fire no matter what extreme methods they use.

If this is what Luke means, then it would make sense for him to put the three men, not in chronological order, but in order of their contribution to God's agenda. He is saying, in other words, that Theudas got a few things right, that Judas's movement was closer and that all of God's plans and agendas have reached their fullness in Jesus and his followers. Let us look closer at the rebellions of these two men to see what they have in common with the ministry of Jesus.

THEUDAS

This is what Josephus has to say about Theudas in his *Antiquities of the Jews*:

> While Fadus was procurator of Judea, a magician named Theudas persuaded many of the people to take their property with them and follow him to the river Jordan, for he told them he was a prophet and that at his command he would divide the river and provide them an easy passage over it. Many were taken in by his words, but Fadus did not let them go on with this madness but sent a troop of cavalry out against them, attacking them unexpectedly and killing many of them while capturing many more alive, including Theudas, whose head they cut off and brought to Jerusalem.[141]

---

[141] Josephus, *Antiquities of the Jews*. 20:97-98

Theudas's activities were centred on the Jordan River. This immediately makes us think of the preaching of John the Baptist who was also based in that region. This may also make us wonder why, if Luke is trying to trace the various movements that led up to the coming of the Christ, he does not include John in the list. He cannot because Gamaliel is supposed to be listing those movements that faded away once their leaders were killed and Luke knows very well that the followers of John did not disappear when he was killed. In a few chapters he will give an account of a faithful follower of John the Baptist who is still preaching many years later than this.[142] As much as he might like to, Luke cannot include John the Baptist's among those movements that led up to Jesus.

Theudas's location at the Jordan River actually points to something else. He seems to have been intent on repeating a famous Old Testament episode where Joshua led the people through the Jordan as it opened before them and they began their conquest of the Promised Land.[143] The content of Theudas's preaching seems quite clear. He was calling the people to begin a new conquest of the land of Israel. Whether he intended that, with God's help, they should free the land from the occupying Romans or from some other impurity or injustice we cannot know. We can, though, understand why the Romans might have perceived Theudas and the large following he gathered out by the river to be a threat.

What is there in this movement of Theudas that Luke might see as a precursor to Jesus and what he came to proclaim? The surprising thing about Theudas is the ease with which the Romans dealt with him. Josephus says that the Governor only had to send one troop of cavalry against them and this was sufficient to kill and capture many of them, including Theudas himself. Such an easy victory for the Romans suggests that Theudas and his followers were completely unarmed. It is perhaps in this nonviolent way of dealing with issues of the day that Luke sees a kinship to Jesus's approach. Luke isn't saying that Theudas understood everything or that he had all the right approaches, but he is saying that he had a few things right and perhaps he is thinking particularly about Theudas rejection of violence.

---

[142] Acts 18:25
[143] Joshua 3

Josephus, in both his *Jewish Wars* and his later *Antiquities of the Jews* has nothing good to say about Judas the Galilean. This is because he sees Judas as the founder of that Jewish sect, the Zealots, that Josephus believes is most to blame for the Jewish Revolt of 66-70 CE. Josephus blames the Zealots for provoking the destruction of the nation by the Romans.

This is how Josephus introduces Judas in his *Jewish Wars*:

> Archelaus's territory was reduced to an eparchy
> and Coponius, a Roman knight, was quickly sent as
> procurator, entrusted by Caesar with the power of
> life and death. Under him a Galilean named Judas
> incited his people to rebel, calling them cowards if
> they paid tax to the Romans and let themselves be
> ruled by mortal men, having formerly served God
> alone. This deceiver had his own sect, quite
> different from the others.[144]

Several years later, in his *Antiquities of the Jews*, Josephus gives more details on what Judas did and heaps more scorn on his methods.

> But Judas, a Gaulonite from a city called Gamala,
> with the support of the Pharisee Sadduc, stirred
> them to revolt by calling this taxation nothing but
> an introduction to slavery and urging the nation to
> reassert its freedom. This would allow them to
> regain prosperity and retain their own property, as
> well as something still more valuable, the honour
> and glory of acting with courage. They said that
> God would surely help them to achieve their goals,
> if they set their hearts on great ideals and not grow
> tired in carrying them out. What they said was
> eagerly listened to and great progress was made in
> this bold project, so that indescribable troubles
> came on the nation as a result of these men. We
> were embroiled in interminable violence and war,
> and lost the friends who could alleviate our misery,
> when our leading men were robbed and murdered,
> under the pretext of the common good, but in

---

[144] Josephus, *The Jewish War* 2:117-118.

reality for private gain. From them came the seeds of political murder, for the mania for victory sometimes caused people to kill their own race, wanting none of the opposition to survive any more than their enemies. The revolt brought famine upon us and utter despair, as our cities were taken and demolished, until even the temple of God was burned down by our enemies.[145]

Although Josephus has set us up to believe that Judas, Sadduc and their associates were capable of any kind of atrocity, when he actually comes a few paragraphs later to describe the actual crimes that they committed, we get a very different picture.

> Judas the Galilean was the originator of the fourth way of Jewish philosophy, which agrees in most things with the views of the Pharisees, but is intensely devoted to freedom and claims God as the only Ruler and Lord. They are prepared for any kind of death, and even accept the deaths of relatives and friends, rather than call any man lord. Since their immovable resolve is well known to many, I shall say no more about it, nor do I fear that what I have said of them will be disbelieved. What I do fear is that I have understated the indifference they show in the face of misery and pain.[146]

When it comes right down to it, Josephus, as much as he might like to, cannot pin any murders or violence on Judas and his followers. In fact, the only deaths he can blame them for are their own and the deaths of their friends and families. They are not killing; they are *being killed* by the Romans or other authorities. What Josephus is describing here is a group of people who are willing to die and even to allow their friends and relatives to die for what they believe but who are, apparently, not willing to kill for it. They are willing to suffer much pain, but not willing to inflict it. This clearly seems to be a description of a non-violent resistance.

John Dominic Crossan, in his book *God and Empire*, makes an excellent argument that Judas the Galilean and his followers were

---

[145] Josephus, *Antiquities of the Jews* 18:4-8
[146] Josephus, *Antiquities of the Jews* 18:23-25

110

essentially non-violent. I will not repeat his full argument here but will add his final point:

> Whenever armed revolts broke out in the Jewish homeland, some or all of the four Roman legions stationed near Antioch on the Orontes to guard the Euphrates frontier marched southward for brutal and punitive suppression. But they did not move from their Syrian base camps against Judas and his followers. That confirms for me that their resistance was nonviolent and could therefore be handled by the prefect's own police forces and auxiliary troops. Thus Judas, not Jesus, was the first Galilean to proclaim nonviolent resistance to violent injustice in the first quarter of the first century CE.[147]

The essential non-violence of Judas is papered over by Josephus who tends to lump all of those who are actively resisting the rule of Rome into one group: the Zealots. Some of these rebels—such as the *Sicarii* who used assassination to overwhelm the people with fear in the years leading up to the Jewish Revolt—were indeed terrorists and quite worthy, in my opinion, of all Josephus's scorn. Others, such as Theudas and Judas, were different. They were not violent and didn't use terror as a tool.

Nevertheless, they were completely dedicated to their cause. You could arrest them, kill their leaders and break up the groups, but they would not disappear. Particular groups may have faded away for a while in the face of oppression, but somehow the ideas they represented just kept coming back and getting stronger and building towards... what? Perhaps Luke believes that it has all been building up to Jesus and his followers. Theudas may have gotten some parts of the non-violent doctrine right. And Judas may have had a greater grasp of God's overall plan. But in Jesus, God's kingdom has finally appeared in such a way that it will never recede no matter what the authorities may do to restrain it.

Could that be what Luke is trying to say through the voice of the revered elder Gamaliel? I don't know, but I believe it is possible. It certainly suggests that we ought to look more closely at the insurrection of Judas the Galilean.

---

[147] John Dominic Crossan, *God and Empire*, HarperSanFranciso, 2007. p. 94.

INTERLUDE: A COUNCIL OF THE RESISTANCE

The rebel leader stands looking south over the Galilean hills towards Judea. He sees heavy dark clouds moving in from the sea. There will be a storm and it will be a big one but he doesn't think that it will strike this far north. In any case, that is not the storm that worries him. The clouds are sent by God and God will let their rains fall on the good or the evil as he wills.

But there is another storm that brews to the south and this one concerns him deeply because he is certain that Galilee will not be spared its wrath for long.

His most trusted lieutenant, a Pharisee named Zadok, comes up behind him. "Peace be with you, Judas," he says in the traditional greeting of his people.

"Ah, Zadok, my friend, there will be no peace—not for our people—not so long as the Romans can do what they like in our land. You've heard what they're planning, I suppose."

"You mean the census they are taking down in Judea?"

"It is not just the census," replies Judas the Galilean turning to face the Pharisee, "It is everything that goes with it. They have taken over the government of the entire country. Do you realize that it will be a Roman governor who sits in the palace at Jerusalem from now on? I know that we detested Herod and his sons. I know that they were not truly Jews and only pretended to share our faith, but at least they understood us. How will our land bear it if our holy city is ruled by a Roman?

"But that is not the worst part. They are also imposing a new tax—a head tax, they call it. If the tax is imposed in Judea and it goes unchallenged there, you know very well that it will be demanded of the

Galileans too. You know as well as I do that our people cannot even afford the taxes that they pay now.

"Just today I had another family come in and join our band. They lost their land because they couldn't pay their taxes and feed their children at the same time. They went into debt and then when they couldn't repay, they lost everything. They came to us because they refused to be sold as slaves. They had no place else to go and I could not turn them away."

"You are right, my brother," replies Zadok. "What is happening in this land is against all of God's laws. God surely wants his people to dwell in safety, to live on their land and to live by the goods that it produces.

"If only this country that God gave us were still governed by God's laws all of this would be set right. The year of jubilee would be proclaimed and every Israelite man would be able to reclaim his birthright—his land and his freedom. But that will never happen—not so long as the Romans rule here."

Judas looks sharply at his friend. "Are you certain, Zadok? Do you know in your heart that it is God's will that there be a jubilee?"

"Of that I have no doubt whatsoever," Zadok replies. "But who will proclaim such a year? Not the Romans. And not Herod Antipas either. He is as bad as they are."

"If it is God's will," Judas says thoughtfully, "surely it need not wait for such people to make it happen."

"What are you suggesting?" Zadok's heart begins to race at the sheer audacity of what he thinks his friend is saying. "Who do you think should proclaim such a jubilee?"

Judas puts his arm around the Pharisee's shoulders. "I'm glad you asked me that. Let us gather our company. We have a great deal to talk about."

A council is held. The leaders talk late into the night. Many are sceptical of Judas's proposal. They do not doubt that it is God's will that a jubilee be proclaimed, but they doubt that the people will believe and respond to such a proclamation coming from a group such as theirs.

Judas is persuasive and the people respect and honour his conviction, knowing that he is truly committed to a better life for all the people.

7) THE CALL TO JUBILEE

The year 6 CE—the year in which Luke portrays Jesus as being born—was a very interesting year in Judea and Galilee. A great deal was happening.

Judea was being formally absorbed into the Roman Empire. After decades spent as a client kingdom—one step removed from direct Roman rule—it would now be directly administered by Roman officials. As an initial step in this full integration a census of the entire province was taken.

Another change occurred in that year. A new tax was imposed on the people of Judea called the *tributum capitis*—a head tax. Henk Jagersma suggests that it was this new tax, more than anything else, which provoked the greatest opposition, as it imposed a particularly heavy burden on the population of Syria and Judea.[148]

Galilee, ruled by the Roman client and *tetrarch* Herod Antipas, was not directly affected by these events in Judea. But, owing to their geography and their large Jewish population, the Galileans were obviously very interested. The census became the flashpoint for all of the discontent with the Roman occupation and especially the unjust tax system. This discontent manifested itself in a rebellion centred in Galilee and led by a Galilean named Judas.

We do not know exactly what areas were impacted by this rebellion. But the fact that its leader was known as "the Galilean" indicates that there was some association with that territory. It must have had some impact on Judea and Samaria in the south but it would not be surprising if the insurgents based themselves within Galilee, hiding behind some of the bureaucratic protections that Antipas's administration offered them, much to Antipas's chagrin, of course, and conducting operations across the borders.

In the year 6 CE it must have been a time when the whole idea of jubilee was on a lot of people's minds. The Roman economic policies were pushing people into debt and often into foreclosure. People were losing the lands that had been in their families for generations. In times past, such a situation would have been remedied eventually by a jubilee year. But, as we have already seen, in that year the jubilee had lost its power to remedy anything. Hillel's *prosbul* legislation, which effectively invalidated the jubilee

---

[148] H. Jagersma, p. 119.

law, was passed by the Sanhedrin sometime between 30 BCE and 10 CE.

Unfortunately, we cannot be any more precise than that with the date of the legislation. All that we know is that the law was proposed by Hillel and that Hillel was active on the council between those dates. There are two possibilities: either it was at that very time—in 6 CE—that the new legislation was working its way through the Sanhedrin, putting it on everyone's mind, or the legislation had been passed a decade or two earlier and in 6 CE the effects of the new clause inserted in contracts were finally being felt as people realized that they could never again hope for economic relief in the form of a jubilee. Either way, many people must have been thinking about the idea of a jubilee in the year of the census.

We have already discovered that the revolt of Judas the Galilean took the form of nonviolent resistance. That assertion forces us to ask a question: how could an insurgency based in Galilee have non-violently resisted a census that was not even taking place in that jurisdiction? They couldn't resist by refusing to be counted or by giving false information. The Romans weren't counting Galileans anyway!

But a unique method of resistance may have presented itself to them as they reflected on the idea of a jubilee.

ZADOK THE PHARISEE

In his *Antiquities of the Jews*, Josephus says that Judas the Galilean was aided in his rebellion by a Pharisee named Sadduc.[149] This is, in fact, a rather strange thing for Josephus to say, for he also claims that Judas was the founder of a "fourth philosophy" of Judaism which he sets in opposition to the three others including the school of the Pharisees. Yet he also says that Sadduc, a Pharisee, helped found this movement.

The name *Sadduc* is quite meaningful. It is the Greek form of the Hebrew name Zadok and it was likely by this Hebrew name that the man was known to the people of his time. Zadok was the name of the priest appointed by King David and the founder of an important priestly dynasty.[150] The name comes from a Hebrew word that means "righteous" or "just." It is also the word that is the root of the name of one of the other sects that Josephus mentions called

[149] Josephus, *Antiquities of the Jews* 18:4.
[150] 2 Samuel 8:17

the Sadducees. A man with such a symbolically significant name may have been a great asset to Judas's movement. His presence among the leadership may have reassured some who were hesitant to see God's hand in what Judas was doing.

This is all that we know about Zadok, his name and that he was a Pharisee, but it is enough to identify Zadok as a religious leader and to remind us that Judas's movement was not just about political or economic goals. It was also deeply spiritual and tied to issues that were connected to Israel's longstanding relationship with its God.

We, as modern people, have a tendency to make a sharp separation between spiritual matters on the one hand and secular matters on the other. Ancient people did not make that separation. The sacred and the secular, as we would call them, blended together in all areas of daily life and this was perhaps especially true for Jews. Judas and Zadok and all those who were with them could not have conceived of an insurrection that was not at one and the same entirely spiritual and entirely political.

A Spiritual Revolt

What, exactly, were the spiritual dimensions of their revolt? Josephus writes only this:

> A Galilean named Judas incited his people to rebel, calling them cowards if they paid tax to the Romans and let themselves be ruled by mortal men, having formerly served God alone.[151]

And he adds in the *Antiquities:*

> But Judas, a Gaulonite from a city called Gamala, with the support of the Pharisee Sadduc, stirred them to revolt by calling this taxation nothing but an introduction to slavery and urging the nation to reassert its freedom. This would allow them to regain prosperity and retain their own property, as well as something still more valuable, the honour and glory of acting with courage. They said that God would surely help them to achieve their goals, if they set their hearts on great ideals and not grow tired in carrying them out.[152]

---

[151] Josephus, *The Jewish War* 2:118.
[152] Josephus, *Antiquities of the Jews* 18:4, 5.

From what Josephus tells us, these Galileans did see their revolt as a religious duty—a way of affirming that their primary obedience was to God and not to Rome. They also believed that, since God had set them free, they should not be slaves to anyone—that they were to be God's slaves alone. Most interesting, they believed that God would help them to "regain prosperity and *retain their own property.*"

Where would these people have gotten the impression that it was God's plan for them that they be freed from slavery and they be able to retain their own (ancestral) property? It is not hard to see how they came to believe that God wanted them to be free from slavery. There are many passages in the Old Testament that speak of God setting his people free. Perhaps the Passover story is the best example.[153] But, given that most of the slavery in Palestine at the time was caused by indebtedness, it is quite possible that the particular passage in the Bible that led them to this belief was none other than Leviticus 25 where God's desire that his people should be free from debt slavery is made very explicit with concrete and practical measures. It is also notable that, in that passage, freedom from slavery is tied to the idea of God's ownership of all the people. God says, "They and their children with them shall go free in the jubilee year. For *to me the people of Israel are servants; they are my servants* whom I brought out from the land of Egypt: I am the LORD your God."[154] This is very similar to the rhetoric of the rebel group as reported to us by Josephus.

Where would Judas, Zadok and their associates have gotten the idea that it was God's will that they be able to retain their ancestral properties? I can think of only one Old Testament passage that could have led them to that conclusion—the jubilee law: "What was sold shall remain with the purchaser until the year of jubilee; in the jubilee it shall be released, and the property shall be returned."[155]

It seems, therefore, that there is evidence in Josephus's works that these rebels did have the idea of a jubilee on their minds. Why wouldn't they? The economic policies of the Romans were putting so many Judeans and Galileans under a great deal of pressure— driving them into debt, forcing many of them to lose their properties and their freedom. And, because of the recent (or current) *prosbul* legislation in the Sanhedrin, these people had lost (or were losing) the legal protection from such eventualities that their

---

[153] Exodus 12
[154] Leviticus 25:54, 55. Emphasis added.
[155] Leviticus 25:28

ancestors had long enjoyed. It would not be surprising at all if at such a moment the refrain, "We need a jubilee," was found upon many lips in Judea and Galilee.

But there was no one with proper authority proclaiming the needed jubilee and, thanks to Hillel's law, no one would ever do it again. It seems quite conceivable, therefore, that a group of rebellion minded people, like the group around Judas and Zadok, could have decided that, if a jubilee was needed most, they would go ahead and proclaim a jubilee themselves.

Of course, since these people had no political authority to make the proclamation, it would have to be a proclamation like the one made in Isaiah 61:1-3. Just as that prophet had no authority to make the rich and the powerful observe a jubilee, Judas and Zadok had no political authority. Like that ancient prophet they, too, may have believed that "the Spirit of the Lord" had given them all the authority they needed to proclaim it anyway.

Since only the poorest people would be likely to respond to such a call, such a proclamation of jubilee would only lead to one particular response. The first thing that was to happen in a year of jubilee was this: "In this year of jubilee you shall return, every one of you, to your property."[156] And this was the only command that was to be observed by everyone. All the other commands placed the burden of obedience on wealthy slave owners and landholders. A jubilee that was only observed by the lowest elements of society in the midst of a census would have looked something like this: "All went to their own towns to be registered."[157]

Most importantly, there would have been a political point to taking even just such communal action. It would have played great havoc with the Romans and their census. Josephus states elsewhere that "Judas… persuaded many of the Jews not to submit to taxation when Quirinius was sent to collect it in Judea."[158] This makes it clear that disrupting the census was one of his goals. But how could a Galilean affect a census that was taking place in another jurisdiction? A jubilee—creating a mass migration of people—offers an excellent method for disruption.

Since the rebellion was centred in Galilee and yet was brought on by the census that was taking place next door in Judea, we can just imagine how this might have happened. Hundreds, maybe thousands, of Galileans headed into Judean territories to register

---

[156] Leviticus 25:13
[157] Luke 2:3
[158] Josephus, *The Jewish War*, 7:253.

and to make their claims of ownership of lands in that territory. Many of these claims would have been legitimate ancestral claims like Joseph's (legitimate, that is, according to the ancient Mosaic law, not Roman law). It is also likely that some others were content to make bogus claims. They would also have sought to persuade many Judeans not to register or to register fraudulently. Once the claims had been registered, the Galileans could simply disappear back home. And then, later, when the tax collectors came to use the census rolls to collect the taxes on various properties they would find themselves dealing with maddeningly confusing errors. It would be a small victory over the power of Rome, but one that would have been satisfying enough for many.

The other thing that Josephus says about the religious motivations of the rebels is that they refused to "be ruled by mortal men, having formerly served God alone." They saw their rebellion as a way to affirm their obedience to God instead of human authority. If Caesar had ordered that the people be registered in a census and the people dared not refuse that command, how could the rebels make their point that they owed their highest obedience to God and not to the emperor? For them to declare that God had called for a jubilee and then proceed to organize a massive migration of people in obedience to that call, would have given them an opportunity to demonstrate very publically that they served God instead of the emperor. There was a good chance that the Romans, who were often caught off guard by Jewish religious practices, would simply be confused by the whole thing.

Two Galileans Caught up in it All

As long as we are only speculating, it seems that the idea of a jubilee held at the same time as the census might be an historical possibility. It could well be one of the non-violent methods that the rebels used to show their displeasure with Roman rule and economic policies in the Jewish homeland.

If Luke sets his story of the birth of Jesus against the backdrop of the census of 6 CE and also in the midst of a general Galilean insurrection as he indicates in Acts 5:37, we can also speculate on how he would have seen these two expectant Galilean parents reacting to these events. Would Mary and Joseph have responded to a jubilee proclamation made by the rebel Judas and his Pharisee friend Zadok? Would they have accepted that such a call to observe a jubilee truly came from God? And if so, would they have been obedient to God's call by making a risky journey to Joseph's ancestral home in Bethlehem?

We cannot know for sure that it happened that way, but the possibility is intriguing and it certainly gives us a different perspective on the journey that Luke tells us Mary and Joseph made. No longer is it merely made in humble obedience to Caesar's commands. It is still a story of obedience but the primary obedience that the couple gives is to God and God's commands.

The man just rides into the centre of the village and starts blowing on the shofar—the ram's horn. It gives a mighty peal that echoes over the small houses and structures. Nothing ever happens in Nazareth, so you can be sure that it does not take long for every resident to come and gather around him, eager for news—eager to hear whatever he has to say.

As soon as the crowd has formed, the stranger begins to speak.

"I have been sent to every Jewish village and town in Galilee to make this proclamation. The year of jubilee is come—the year of God's justice and of a land set right. In this year of jubilee you shall return, every one of you, to your ancestral property—the land that God gave to your families."

A few make sounds of scorn and derision for they had never expected to hear anyone make such a proclamation in their lifetimes. After some muttering, one of the chief residents of the village speaks up, "And who proclaims this jubilee?" he asks. "By whose authority is it being held?"

"By heaven's!" the man shouts. "The Lord's authority is the only authority that we recognize. And the Lord has laid his spirit upon Judas of Gamala and also upon Zadok the Pharisee to show them his will in this matter."

A murmur runs through the group at the mention of these names. The people know that they are considered to be outlaws by the Romans and by Herod Antipas. Anyone who even associates with them is placed in grave danger. There is word that some have lost their homes and even their lives for protecting members of their rebel band, and so there is considerable fear in the crowd.

But the murmuring also carries another current. It is a note of defiance and even of hope, particularly among those in Nazareth who have lost so much—who have become slaves or day labourers because their debts pushed them off their land.

Most of the people move away from the stranger casting fearful glances over their shoulders. They know that if they are even seen with the man there could be severe consequences.

A few are not so wise. They form a tight knot around the man, peppering him with questions. Most of those who stay are those who have little to lose. They are day labourers and indentured servants. One of them is a local artisan, Joseph the son of Heli. He is the one who seems most engaged in the exchange.

The stranger talks with the brave few until he is confident that they understand what this proclamation means and what risks they will be taking by responding to it. Then he turns his animal to ride off, sounding the shofar as he goes. In between blasts he continues to cry out, "It is the jubilee—the year of God's favour."

Later, when Mary finally catches up with Joseph, she sees a light in his eyes that she has never detected before.

"You're going to Judea, aren't you," she says.

"I must. Something inside me tells me that it is God's will that I go and state my claim to what God has given my family. I dare not disobey the call of God."

"Well, if you are going, I'm coming too."

"But you can't—you mustn't, Mary. It is too dangerous. The roads are not safe. The whole countryside is in an uproar. And you surely cannot travel so far with the baby on its way.

"No, you'll have to stay with your family. They will take care of you and keep you safe. I will return soon enough to greet my son once I have completed the pilgrimage."

"Joseph, you are not the only one who must follow God's commands. I am the servant of the Lord and him only will I serve. I will be a slave to no man and serve none but my husband! That's what the jubilee is all about, isn't it? If I am to be your wife then I am part of your family. It is as simple as that. The command to obey God's call is on me too."

"But the baby…"

"The baby is in God's hands as he has always been. He is a child of destiny and his Father in heaven will not allow anything to happen to him. Somehow it just seems right that he should be born on such a holy pilgrimage."

The couple discuss the matter long into the night, but Mary will not be moved from her convictions. When, two days later, Joseph has made all his preparations and is ready to leave, Mary is with him. He would have liked to have obtained a donkey or some pack animal to ease Mary's journey, but he simply did not have the means. Mary will have to walk alongside him.

She is a strong woman of hardy peasant stock. She assures him that she will manage. They both know that the journey ahead of them will be hard, but they feel a lightness inside them that comes from being obedient to the voice of God.

8) What is Truth?

In the Gospel of John, the great conflict between the power of Rome and the very different kind of power that Jesus represents is portrayed in an extended discussion between the Roman Governor, Pontius Pilate, and Jesus. The discussion ends like this:

> Pilate asked him, "So you are a king?" Jesus answered, "You say that I am a king. For this I was born, and for this I came into the world, to testify to the truth. Everyone who belongs to the truth listens to my voice." Pilate asked him, "What is truth?"[159]

Pilate's final question is just as important today as it ever was. What is truth and who has the authority to decide what is true and what is not? As modern people, we have fallen into the habit of confusing the truth with facts. This is a scientific concept of truth—that truth is only what can be verified by collecting and studying empirical facts and events. Because of this mode of thinking, most modern people, if they ask whether a particular Gospel story is true or not, are really asking whether or not the events related in the story actually happened in the way that it says that they happened.

This modern concept of truth is a good concept of truth. It has helped us to make wonderful scientific advances and to better understand the events of history that have made our society what it is. It has created the standards of journalism on which we depend to understand the events that take place in our world. It has also conditioned us to think about truth in this one particular way.

Modern people, as a rule, are just like Sergeant Friday in Dragnet: they are interested in "just the facts, ma'am," because they believe that it is in the facts that the truth lies. But this modern concept of truth is indeed a modern invention. Ancient people did not think of truth in such restrictive terms. And, since they were ancient people, this also is true of the people who wrote the Christian gospels.

Ancient evangelists would never have been satisfied with merely reporting the facts and events of Jesus's life and death because, as far as they were concerned, they could not communicate the whole truth about Jesus by merely retelling the facts. The truth about Jesus

---

[159] John 18:37, 38

was far bigger than the sum total of all the things that had happened to him. This is why they did not hesitate to change the story in order to make sure that this truth was communicated.

We must remember that the thing that makes the Bible *scripture* is not its ability to record historical events accurately. We believe that the Bible is *scripture* because it is inspired by God. Some people seem to think that the only way that such inspiration works is in making sure that the writers got the historical details correct—that the Holy Spirit acts in the writers of the Bible only in order to allow them to remember what happened accurately or to inform them of details that they cannot know by any other means. I am sure that most of the people who wrote the Bible did not see themselves as mere recorders of what actually happened. They believed that the Spirit gave them the power not only to report but also to interpret the events and, since they were inspired, they did not hesitate to include their interpretations right in the account. Since the interpretation had come from God's Holy Spirit, it had to be just as true as the facts of what had happened.

In John's Gospel, there is a long discourse on the work of the Holy Spirit in the leaders of the church. It contains the promise that God's Spirit will assist the disciples and leaders of the church in maintaining and passing on Jesus's message. Jesus promises that "the Advocate, the Holy Spirit, whom the Father will send in my name, will teach you everything, and *remind* you of all that I have said to you."[160] But the work of the Spirit is certainly not restricted to reminding the disciples of exactly what was said or done. Jesus also goes on in that discourse to say:

> "I still have many things to say to you, but you
> cannot bear them now. When the Spirit of truth
> comes, he will guide you into all the truth; for he
> will not speak on his own, but will speak whatever
> he hears, and he will declare to you the things that
> are to come. He will glorify me, because he will
> take what is mine and declare it to you. All that the
> Father has is mine. For this reason I said that he
> will take what is mine and declare it to you."[161]

In effect, the promise seems to be here that the Spirit will enable Jesus followers not only to remember what he said but also what he *would have said* had they been able to hear it—to remember

---

[160] John 14:26. Emphasis added.
[161] John 16:12-14

126

what he should have said but didn't'. There was therefore an expectation built into the gospel writing process—an expectation in the writers themselves—that the work of the Spirit in the minds and hearts of the writers would lead them to proclaim truths that went beyond what had happened and what had been said during the life of Jesus.

The evangelists were not bound by the modern rules of journalism. The job of a journalist is to present an account of what happened in a certain event and to present that account as objectively as possible. The job of an evangelist is to use the events that happened to present the truth about Jesus—a truth that is subjective; indeed that demands a subjective response.

An Example: The Sermons in Matthew's Gospel

We have already noted in passing one example of how this works. Matthew, in his gospel, presents the teachings of Jesus in a series of five long sermons spread throughout his gospel. These are the famous Sermon on the Mount, a sermon giving instructions for mission, a collection of parables, some teachings about living as a Christian community and a discourse on the end of the age.[162] Most of the content of these Matthean sermons (the sayings and the parables of Jesus) can be found in slightly different forms in the other Biblical gospels. They are even found in other ancient Christian documents such as the *Didache* and the *Gospel of Thomas* but in different contexts. This has led many to the conclusion that Matthew has taken various sayings of Jesus that have come down to him from his sources and the traditions of the church and edited them into these five different extended sermons.

There is no reason to think that Matthew did this because he actually believed or had any particular information that Jesus had actually preached these sermons in exactly these ways on these occasions. Had he just seen himself as a journalist whose job it was simply to present the events of Jesus's life as they had occurred, he would have felt bound to present all of what Jesus had said as disjointed sayings because that was how the material came to him. But Matthew did not see himself as a journalist. He wanted to present the truth about Jesus and his teachings and what they meant

---

[162] 1) Matthew 5,6,7; 2) Matthew 10; 3) Matthew 13; 4) Matthew 18; and 5) Matthew 24,25

as clearly as possible. And so he took those various sayings of Jesus and edited them together into these sermons.

It was a very successful approach. For one thing, the resulting sermons are extraordinarily powerful. There is a good reason why the Sermon on the Mount has touched so many people so deeply down through the centuries. Matthew managed, in a truly inspired way, to combine the sayings of Jesus and enhance their power and meaning in the process. By doing this, he was able to bring out the truth that was there in the words of Jesus and present it to us more forcefully and meaningfully.

Matthew was also doing something else with his editing of Jesus's words. He was presenting Jesus as a new Moses, a new lawgiver offering his new law from a mountaintop and leaving, as a legacy, his five "books" of teachings. We would have been left much poorer if we had missed out on this unique perspective on the ministry of Jesus.

DID IT REALLY HAPPEN?

The gospel writers present truth according to their standards of truth. We need to understand that this is how they operate. If we come to them with an expectation that they will behave as a modern journalist or historian would behave, we are bound to be disappointed sooner or later. They will eventually fail to present the events exactly as they occurred and we will be left with undeniable evidence that they have done so. What will we do then? Either we will be forced to insist, against the evidence, that they are being completely accurate down to the last detail or we will lose faith in the gospel accounts entirely, dismissing it all as a pack of lies.

It seems to be the choice that many Christians feel that they have to make today. But does it really have to be so stark? So long as we are judging the gospel accounts according to the modern standards of truth, they will necessarily fail. When we judge them according to the standards of their own time, the gospels prove themselves repeatedly to be remarkably truthful.

There is no way to prove historically that Jesus was born at a particular time, in a particular place or under certain circumstances. You cannot demonstrate that he was born of a virgin, laid in a manger or visited by shepherds. The best you can do is argue that the gospel writers have given their stories a plausible historical setting. Luke has done that—the setting of the birth during a census that we know happened and in the midst of a jubilee observance that could have happened makes it seem authentic, but that is hardly proof that it did happen in the way that he says.

We cannot know how Luke came to set the birth within the context that he did. Perhaps he started by researching the events that took place around the time that he calculated that Jesus had been born. He probably didn't have a specific date of birth when he began, just a vague notion that Jesus must have been born about 30 years before he was crucified.[163] But, as he did his research, Luke learned about some of the events that took place in and around 6 CE: a census, Judea's incorporation into the empire, a new tax, a rebellion and perhaps even an attempt to observe the jubilee on the part of some. This historical information had a profound effect on Luke. He began to imagine Jesus's birth taking place among all of these events and could not deny the deep meaning and significance that such an historical context would have given the start of his messiah's life. And once he started imagining it, it would not have taking much persuasion (or prompting from the Holy Spirit) to come to the conclusion the Jesus *must* have been born in the midst of all those events. And so he wrote his account.

If that is how Luke decided on the historical setting of the birth, there would be no problem identifying the process that brought Luke to conclude that Jesus was born in that year as an inspired process. He certainly would have understood that it was the presence of the Holy Spirit that allowed his mind to leap to such conclusions. Who can argue that God's Spirit was not present in such an extraordinary chain of thought?

What did Luke think about the account even as he wrote it? Did he think that the events that he was recounting actually happened exactly as he was saying? Such a question would have never even occurred to Luke. He was doubtlessly confident that the words that he was writing were true because he was confident that the Holy Spirit was inspiring those words. He really had no need to think beyond such confidence, and his confidence in the Spirit's leading is ultimately the only proof that he can offer us.

It may not be a satisfying answer for modern people like us, but it may be the only answer that we can get. Luke was satisfied to know that the story was true according to his standards of truth and knowledge. We need to decide for ourselves how we will accept his proclamation of that truth.

---

[163] Luke 3:23

After studying at length the story of the birth of Jesus that Luke offers us, I appreciate how the author has gone to great lengths to tell the story within a meaningful historical context. His use of history has fired my imagination and made the story seem much more realistic. Of course I would like to think that it all really happened in manner that I have imagined, but I cannot know that it did. For Luke, that was not the point of his narrative.

For Luke, what made it true was its proclamation of the truth about Jesus—who he was, what his coming meant and what it accomplished. If we really want to come to grips with the truth in the nativity story of Luke, those are the things that we need to understand in his account. That is how the author intended us to find the authenticity in his nativity story.

What did Luke really intend to say about the incarnation— about the coming of Jesus into this world—by setting his birth in the midst of the census of 6 CE, in the midst of a rebellion against Rome in Galilee and in the context of a jubilee observance by the poor people of Galilee and Judea? If we can answer that question, we can begin to find Luke's truth in this account.

By setting Jesus's birth in such circumstances, Luke seems to plunge right into some of the most controversial questions of that age. Given that the Roman occupation of Palestine had devastating consequences for many people who lived in that region, what was an appropriate response? What could they or should they do about all the wrong that came with Roman rule? This had to be something that an enormous number of Jews in that age agonized over.

In many ways they didn't have a choice. They had to live inside the empire and they had to follow its laws and work within its systems. At the same time they felt a strong need to set themselves apart from the empire and its ways and to protest against its most devastating policies. They particularly needed to declare that they owed their highest obedience to God and not to the emperor. The empire was always reminding the people in its inscriptions and proclamations that the emperor was a god, the son of a god and the only one to whom they could turn to find salvation and peace. Jews and early Christians did not accept such ideas even though they were generally accepted by the people who surrounded them but did not have safe ways to express their dissent.

The situation set up a hard choice. Would they obey the emperor or would they obey God? Luke sends the key characters in the birth narrative, Mary and Joseph, into the heart of this difficult choice. He declares them to be obedient to the orders of an emperor to be registered in a census. But he also introduces a hint that they are obedient to something else—to a call to observe a jubilee—which indicates that they believe that their highest calling is to serve God alone. Thus Luke allows his protagonists to successfully navigate one of the toughest moral minefields of the age.

A STORY FOR US

These hard decisions did not exist only in the ancient world. As believers today, we are often left struggling with conflicting allegiances. We are believers pledged to follow Jesus and to serve God faithfully but we are also citizens of nations, members of churches, of families and of communities. We have friendships and business relationships. Each one of these relationships demands of us a certain loyalty. How are we to react when one of these other loyalties comes into conflict with our commitment to God? How will we react if our country engages in questionable or immoral actions? How will we react if our community or our employer demands that we do something that we suspect our God would condemn? How, under such circumstance, can we plot a course that maintains our commitment to God?

These moral conflicts and questions are familiar enough to all who try to take their commitment to God seriously despite the fact that they live in this flawed world. I believe that Luke wrote his nativity story in part to help people to sort through those difficult kinds of questions—to help us think creatively about how we can remain obedient to God in a world that demands our obedience to so many other things. Luke is inviting us all, like Joseph, to take up our staff and, like Mary, to head out in obedience to God's law and God's command no matter what Caesar may have to say about it. Let us take up his invitation and imagine what such a journey might look like today.

It is dark, well past midnight, and in the middle of the field where they found the manger, the small family is huddled near a little fire. Joseph sits and watches the infant sleeping in the manger. It is a boy, just like Mary had assured him it would be—a tiny little boy who sleeps contentedly for the moment, his stomach full of milk.

Up until this point, Joseph has wondered how he would feel about this child. Would he see him as his own, love him like his own? But now that the boy has arrived—now that he has held him in his arms— any doubts that Joseph ever had have simply been swept away. He knows in his heart that this child will be his son in every way that matters. He will love him with all his heart.

The boy's mother also sleeps, rolled in a blanket nearby, taking advantage of the brief respite from the babe's demands. Joseph, though he has every reason to be exhausted, finds that he is wide awake.

It is a beautiful night, the stars blaze down from a moonless, cloudless sky and he is content to simply marvel at the sight of the child sleeping and watch his little chest rising and falling underneath the swaddling clothes.

Suddenly the babe stirs. He grimaces and for a moment Joseph fears that he is about to wake. He knows that if the child wails, his mother will wake and he knows how tired she is. He reaches for the boy. "Sh-shalom," he whispers. "Peace, child, let your mother sleep."

He picks up the child, paces with him a bit and is relieved to see him settle back into a contented sleep. But still he whispers the word over and over again. "Shalom, shalom..."

Peace...

There were some local shepherds who came by earlier this night telling wild stories of heavenly angels and bright lights and terror in the night. They were very excited and Joseph understood little of what they said, though Mary nodded and smiled at them as if she knew exactly what they were talking about.

But there was one thing they said that has stayed with Joseph. They spoke about peace—peace on earth and people of good will. They said it was part of the angelic message.

Joseph has never thought all that much about peace. He has always seen it as a Roman thing, something that had little to do with him. You see, the Romans are always talking about peace—the pax romanum they call it. They are constantly promising and proclaiming that the very purpose of the empire is to create peace on earth.

But when they talk about peace, what they really mean is that, once they have defeated all of their enemies, no one will be left who is strong enough to resist whatever they want to do. Joseph has always taken such "peace" for granted. It is one of the facts of life in Galilee. It is the kind of peace that constantly reminds him that there really is nothing he can do to change the way the world works.

He has always had mixed feelings about such peace. He does grudgingly appreciate the stability that Roman rule brings but cannot stop wondering about the cost that comes with Roman domination.

Peace...

Sitting here, watching the child sleep and thinking of the strange words of the shepherds, he wonders if there couldn't be another kind of peace—one that doesn't come at the point of a sword—a peace from heaven.

He looks back across the field towards the house which is now dark. Joseph has come a long way to get to set his feet upon this little corner of God's earth. The road has certainly not been easy. Why did he do it? Why did he bring Mary on such a perilous path? He had thought that he was coming to find God's jubilee—to find it in a piece of land that once belonged to his family. But what he has found surprises him.

He has found his jubilee, but it is not in the land. For some reason, he can sense the presence of jubilee in the boy—a presence so real that it cannot be denied. Somehow when Joseph looks at this helpless infant he cannot help but believe that God will remember his people—that he will not leave them without hope or salvation. The boy, he now realizes, is the real answer to all of the prayers of so many people that have gone up to God asking for a jubilee.

He certainly does not regret having made the journey. It means so much to him that his son was born in this place. Never in his life has he known what it was like to have land that belonged to him. Now he has given to this boy the smallest taste of it and suddenly he can no longer look at the whole matter in quite the same way.

Like any other descendant of Jacob, Joseph believes that the land is a gift of God to all the families of Israel. The gift came, in the ancient days, by means of God's servant Joshua. It came through conquest and battle and violence. That is why Joseph has always assumed that, if the land is ever to be reclaimed for the families of Israel, it will have to be through more violence.

But the words of the shepherds and the sight of this child of promise sleeping so peacefully have made Joseph think differently about such things. Perhaps what they really need now is not for the old Joshua and his ways to return. Perhaps the need is for a new Joshua who will show a new way.

Surprisingly, as far as Joseph is concerned, both he and Mary have individually decided to give their child the same name despite the fact that it is not a common name in either family. Mary hasn't shared her reasons for choosing the name. There are some things about this child that she keeps and ponders only in her own heart, speaking of them to no one. But Joseph has his own reasons for why he thinks their son should be named Joshua.

He had thought that it was because he was looking for the return of the old Joshua and for another war of conquest to take back the land from the Romans and any who support them by force. But now he looks at it differently. He believes that it is time for God to send a different kind of Joshua—one who will restore the land to the families of Israel but will do it in such a way that they might possess it in true peace.

Yes, as a sign of a new hope and great possibilities, Joseph has decided that the boy will be named Joshua. He knows it is the right name for this child. In Aramaic (the common speech of the people), it will be Yeshua.

Joseph doesn't know this, but in Greek—the language spoken throughout the Eastern Empire, the language of Caesar and all his minions—the child's name will mean the same thing but it will sound different.

In Greek, someday, they will call him Jesus.

Luke tells us that on one occasion, near the end of Jesus's life, some people came up to him and asked him a tough question:

> "Teacher, we know that you are right in what you
> say and teach, and you show deference to no one,
> but teach the way of God in accordance with truth.
> Is it lawful for us to pay taxes to the emperor, or
> not?"[164]

Luke describes the question as a trap because no matter what answer Jesus gave it was bound to get him in trouble with someone. The tax they were talking about was the *tributum capitis*, the head tax that was first imposed in 6 CE when Judea was integrated into the empire. The tax was controversial when it was introduced—provoking open revolt—and it certainly remained controversial throughout Jesus's life.

Jesus was in a tough spot. If he endorsed the paying of the tax, that is, if he said that it was in accordance with God's law, he would earn the scorn of many in the community and probably of many of his own followers. If he said that one shouldn't pay it, the authorities would certainly have heard about it and he would have gotten into a lot of trouble very quickly. Who knows, they might have crucified him!

The question was also complicated by the fact that the empire was certainly not all bad. The Roman system brought many benefits with it. It brought improved security and stability. The Romans were famous for their infrastructure projects such as roads, aqueducts and harbours. Even if many of these blessings benefited some more than they did others, and even if the tax burden that supported them was great, the things that the Romans brought were still appreciated.

The greatest benefit that the empire claimed to offer the world was peace: the famous *pax romanum*. Augustus Caesar and his successors maintained that, by taking over the affairs of the Roman Republic, they had put an end to war and strife and brought into being all of the benefits that came with peace and stability. This was true to a certain extent. They certainly had brought to an end the terrible civil wars that worn the very fabric of Roman society to

---

[164] Luke 20:21, 22

shreds for generations. They had also imposed stability and an end to hostilities in the territories Rome occupied. But there was no denying that the Roman peace came to most of the people in the provinces at the point of a sword. Maintaining this peace meant that any voice that was raised in opposition was silenced and any sign of rebellion was put down swiftly and brutally.

So the situation in an occupied Palestine was not simple and blanket condemnations would not have been very helpful. Even the most ardent foes of the empire likely would have had some mixed feelings about their opposition to Roman power. How could Jesus say anything that would capture everyone's feelings about the Roman presence in Judea?

Jesus's answer to this tricky question is justly famous. The first thing that he did was ask to see the coin used to pay the tax. The request was a key part of his answer. It was his way of demonstrating that he didn't have any of these coins that they were talking about. Jesus was making it abundantly clear, in other words, that he didn't carry any money—not even a single coin. Indeed, he even pretended that he is so unfamiliar with the currency that he didn't know whose face was engraved upon the coin. "Show me a denarius," he said. "Whose head and whose title does it bear?"[165]

It is quite impossible, of course, that Jesus didn't know that the emperor's face and title was engraved on the coin. But he more than likely asked the question with a feigned air of ignorance—as if he really didn't know. He was trying to make it very clear to everyone who was listening that the question being asked really didn't have anything to do with him personally.

The question was based on the assumption that everyone participated in the economic system and so had money owing to the emperor in the form of taxes. By never possessing or using money, by engaging in no trade or exchange, Jesus had effectively opted out of that economic system. Jesus had also apparently instructed his followers to live in the same manner by sending them out with these instructions: "Take nothing for your journey, no staff, nor bag, nor bread, nor money—not even an extra tunic."[166] So, in a very real sense, Jesus's answer to this tough question was to say that the question didn't have anything to do with him. The problem was a problem for those who had money, but not for him.

But even if Jesus had, in some sense, opted out of the Roman economic system, he surely knew that it was not possible for

---

[165] Luke 20:24
[166] Luke 9:3

everyone to live in such a radically different way. And so he offered some advice for dealing with a conflict that was inevitable for anyone who owed allegiance to God and yet who still lived within the empire's system. On being told that the coin bore the image of the emperor, Jesus said, "Render therefore unto Caesar the things which be Caesar's, and unto God the things which be God's."[167]

If Jesus didn't have any coins, then he didn't have anything *of* the emperor and so he didn't need to give anything *to* the emperor. Jesus himself did not suffer from any such divided loyalty. Nevertheless, his words suggest that it is possible to navigate this problem—that there is a way to divide the things that are the emperor's from the things that are God's. Unfortunately, Jesus did not go on from there to explain exactly how to sort through all of the things you have in your life and decide what belongs on the "God" pile and what belongs on the "Caesar" pile. Jesus, somewhat typically, left that work to us.

Perhaps Luke was not content to leave the matter there. He felt that his readers needed some help to sort what properly belonged to the emperor from what belonged to God. And so, in the second chapter of his gospel, he thrust Mary and Joseph into the very dilemma that was put forward by Jesus's enemies in the twentieth chapter. The couple had to deal with an order from the emperor to be registered for the purpose of paying the *tributum capitis*. In effect, what Luke was saying was that, before Jesus was required to answer the theoretical question of whether it was legal to pay the tax, his parents were forced to deal with the very same question on the most practical of terms.

By introducing hints into his story that Mary and Joseph were, in fact, observing a jubilee by making the journey to Bethlehem, Luke presents them as successfully sorting the things of Caesar from the things of God. They were caught within a system, the Roman Empire, that was flawed and that could be very evil. They set out on a journey to escape from that system and into the ideal of jubilee. They found their jubilee but not in the traditional way, by actually claiming and holding onto a piece of land that may have once belonged to Joseph's ancestors. Luke would say that they found the jubilee in their newborn son instead.

---

[167] Luke 20:25. The King James Version is used for sentimental reasons.

If we really want to understand the meaning of story of Mary and Joseph's journey from Nazareth to Bethlehem and to find all of the messages that Luke has placed in it for us, what we really need to do is emulate them. That is to say, that we need to be willing to set out from the flawed systems of our own world to seek God's will as they did. Their journey, as presented in the Gospel of Luke, is as symbolic as it is geographic. Our journey will be symbolic too.

What are the flawed systems that we must set out from? We must each answer this question for ourselves, but we cannot delude ourselves into thinking our modern systems have no flaws. Yes, they are, in most cases, far superior to the kind of organized exploitation that existed in the Roman Empire in the first century, but injustice and sometimes pure evil can creep into any of them.

One example comes to mind: the economic system. The modern capitalistic economic system offers us many blessings. It enables prosperity; it encourages innovation and creativity and provides avenues for advancement for people from many different walks of life. It is also a system that can make losers just as easily as it can make winners and, contrary to what we have been promised, the winners are not always the ones who have worked the hardest and the losers are not always the lazy ones. It is a system that feeds upon growth and that demands more and more all the time or else it threatens us with collapse. Like any system, it has its faults and it will not always result in what is right and good for everyone involved.

How are we to deal with the problems and contradictions that come with living in and participating in such an economic system? How can we give to the economy what is the economy's and to God what is God's? I would take Luke's story of the nativity journey as an inspiration. As Mary and Joseph conformed outwardly to the emperor's demands, we will conform to the expectations that come with living within a capitalist society. We will go out and work and earn money, we will participate as consumers, debtors, investors and on many other levels. But just as Mary and Joseph's journey had a very different meaning for them than what any Roman authorities could have imagined, we can also cherish a different goal in and through all our economic activities.

Their goal was jubilee—something quite unattainable in that time and place. But their search for that impossible ideal led them to discover a new understanding of jubilee for their time and for the future. It was a new understanding that came with their child and all he would do and be. In the same way, the goal that we would seek in our hearts might seem to be an impossible ideal, but in the very act of seeking, we ought to expect that the Spirit will lead us to a new understanding of God's justice in our time and place.

If we really want to understand the truth that Luke is trying to proclaim in the story of the journey from Nazareth to Bethlehem, we really have to find some way to join in that journey for ourselves. We need to set out from whatever flawed or compromised systems in which we find ourselves, be they economic systems, systems of oppression or racism or of exploitation of the earth or of other human beings. We will set out from these things on a metaphorical journey toward an ideal. It may even be an ideal that is unattainable in this time and place, but just the act of setting out toward it may help us to find what the holy couple found—to find that our God has the fulfillment of our hopes ready for us, but perhaps not in the form we had expected it.

The couple struggles down the road. The man is carrying a sturdy staff and assisting his wife as she struggles beside him. Her belly is round. She shows every sign of pregnancy and it is quite clear that she is near her time to deliver. The travelling is difficult but the pair does not stop. They continue to trudge down that long and lonely road even in the dark of the night.

They are going to Bethlehem, the city of David. They are going because it is the ancestral home of the man, Joseph. All his life he has heard stories of the land that his family owned there—the land that God had given them so that they might be strong and prosper. He is going to claim that property in the name of God and in accordance with the law of the jubilee. He knows, of course, that they will not give it to him, but he goes to make his claim all the same because it is the year of jubilee and he will make sure that God's demands for justice are heard during this year even if some will not allow their hearts to respond.

The woman places her hand on her belly and stifles a sigh. She is struggling, coming to the end of her strength and she fears that she will not make it to her destination. But she continues on because she knows that the journey is worth it. She knows already that her child will be no ordinary child—that his birth will usher in a new age of God's justice. And so, it is only fitting that he should be born on a jubilee pilgrimage to Joseph's ancestral home. Maybe there will never again be a king who will be brave enough to proclaim the year of God's jubilee—maybe the Romans will rule forever—but because of the birth of her son, she knows that God will find a way to make that year real for her people.

Joseph looks at his wife—his face full of concern. But she lifts her chin in defiance of his concern. And then, despite the extremity of their predicament, the two of them share a mischievous smile.

As they have been walking, there have been signs of the Romans making preparations to take their big census. They have seen administrators and officials scurrying about, the movements of troops to provide security. They understand that it will be one of the most complex operations ever carried out in Judea. And the Romans intend to use the data it produces to strengthen their hold over every aspect of the lives of the people of Judea—to count their goods so that they can plunder them later.

But when Joseph registers his ownership of the place that should be his home but that isn't—that would have been his if it weren't for the policies of people like the Romans—he rather suspects that the information that he gives to Caesar's representatives won't do them much good.

It is a small act of defiance, but one that is very meaningful to them. It gives them the chance to demonstrate what they believe: that the land belongs to God and that God is the one who gives it to his people so they might live and serve him.

They also know that they are not alone in their quest for what is right for God's people. They have seen the small acts of resistance and defiance as they have travelled. They know that the faith of the people that God will be with them and will find a way to bring them hope is still strong. They don't understand all of God's plans, but their confidence of God's leading only grows with every step they take.

And so Mary and Joseph struggle on in a journey that has taken on a great deal of meaning for them.

The eastern horizon turns gray and soon lightens. A new day is dawning.

Brown, R. (1977). *The Birth of the Messiah.* Doubleday.

Crossan, J. D. (1992). *The Historical Jesus.* HarperSanFrancisco.

Crossan, J. D. (2007). *God and Empire.* HarperSanFranciso.

Crossan, John Dominic & Borg, Marcus J. (2009). *The First Christmas.* HarperCollins.

Crossan, John Dominic & Reed, Jonathan L. (2004). *In Search of Paul.* HarperSanFrancisco.

Crossan, John Dominic & Reed, Jonathan L. (2009). *Excavating Jesus.* HarperCollins.

Hudson, M. (1999, February). The Economic Roots of the Jubilee. (H. Shanks, Ed.) *Bible Review.*

Jagersma, H. (1985). *A History of Israel from Alexander the Great to Bar Kochba.* Philadelphia: Fortress Press.

Josephus, F. (2007). *Antiquities of the Jews.* (R. Patrick, Trans.) http://www.biblical.ie/josephus.

Josephus, F. (2007). *The Jewish War.* (R. Patrick, Trans.) http://www.biblical.ie/josephus.

Tuckett, C. (1987). *Methods of Interpretation.* Philadelphia: Fortress Press.

About the Author

The Rev. W. Scott McAndless has been an ordained minister of the Presbyterian Church in Canada for two decades. He presently serves the congregation of St. Andrew's Hespeler Presbyterian Church in Cambridge, ON. Canada. He lives with his wife, two daughters and their dog Minnie in Cambridge.

Personal Blog: revstandrewshespeler.blogspot.ca/

Twitter: @A_noble_theme

24145545R00080

Made in the USA
Charleston, SC
13 November 2013